VISITORS' HISTORIC BRITAIN

THE ISLE OF MAN

STONE AGE TO THE SWINGING SIXTIES

VISITORS' HISTORIC BRITAIN

THE ISLE OF MAN

STONE AGE TO THE SWINGING SIXTIES

MATTHEW RICHARDSON

PEN & SWORD
HISTORY
AN IMPRINT OF PEN & SWORD BOOKS LTD
YORKSHIRE – PHILADELPHIA

First published in Great Britain in 2020
and reprinted in 2021, 2023, 2024 and 2025 by
Pen & Sword History
An imprint of
Pen & Sword Books Limited
Yorkshire - Philadelphia

Copyright © Matthew Richardson, 2020, 2021, 2023, 2024, 2025

ISBN 978 1 52672 0 771

The right of Matthew Richardson to be identified as Author of this work has been asserted by him in accordance with the Copyright, Designs and Patents Act 1988.

A CIP catalogue record for this book is available from the British Library

All rights reserved. No part of this book may be reproduced, transmitted, downloaded, decompiled or reverse engineered in any form or by any means, electronic or mechanical including photocopying, recording or by any information storage and retrieval system, without permission from the Publisher in writing. NO AI TRAINING: Without in any way limiting the Author's and Publisher's exclusive rights under copyright, any use of this publication to "train" generative artificial intelligence (AI) technologies to generate text is expressly prohibited. The Author and Publisher reserve all rights to license uses of this work for generative AI training and development of machine learning language models.

Printed and bound in the UK by CPI Group (UK) Ltd, Croydon, CR0 4YY

The Publisher's authorised representative in the EU for product safety is
Authorised Rep Compliance Ltd., Ground Floor, 71 Lower Baggot Street, Dublin D02 P593, Ireland. www.arccompliance.com

For a complete list of Pen & Sword titles please contact

PEN & SWORD BOOKS LIMITED
47 Church Street, Barnsley, South Yorkshire, S70 2AS, England
E-mail: enquiries@pen-and-sword.co.uk
Website: www.pen-and-sword.co.uk
or
PEN AND SWORD BOOKS
1950 Lawrence Road, Havertown, PA 19083, USA
E-mail: uspen-and-sword@casematepublishers.com
Website: www.penandswordbooks.com

Contents

Acknowledgments		vii
Introduction		ix
Chapter 1	Celts and Vikings	1
Chapter 2	The Middle Ages	15
Chapter 3	The Civil War Era and Eighteenth Century	25
Chapter 4	The Victorians	40
Chapter 5	The TT Races	60
Chapter 6	Wartime and the Swinging Sixties	74
Tour route 1	A Walking Tour of Douglas	95
Tour route 2	Ramsey and the North by Car	104
Tour route 3	Peel and the West by Car	117
Tour route 4	Castletown and the South by Car	132
Notes		145
Bibliography and Further Reading		147
Index		148

Acknowledgments

My thanks firstly go to Roni Wilkinson, of Pen and Sword books, for inviting me to contribute this volume of *Visitors' Historic Britain* to the ongoing series. As always I am extremely grateful to those who have assisted me in the preparation of this volume. Andy Johnson and Allison Fox of Manx National Heritage who assisted with archaeological aspects, and Andy Wint who advised me on Radio Caroline. Frank Cowin assisted with maritime and other aspects. Nevertheless, it goes without saying that any errors of interpretation or fact are my own.

All illustrations contained herewith are from the author's collection, unless otherwise stated.

Introduction

The Isle of Man is located in the Irish Sea, at the geographical centre of the British Isles. It is not, and never has been, a part of the United Kingdom. Instead it is a crown dependency, owing its allegiance directly to the British monarch, who holds the title Lord of Man. The Island's history, though connected with that of the United Kingdom, is separate, and as a result a unique identity, culture and legal/political framework have developed here. The Island is self-governing through its parliament, known as Tynwald, which is stated to be the oldest continuous political assembly in the world. The crown is represented on the Island by a Lieutenant-Governor, whose roles and functions are now largely symbolic. Though geographically small, the Island has at many times played a disproportionately significant part in British history.

Many visitors are amazed to discover the sheer number of 'oldests', 'and 'firsts' associated with the Isle of Man. Though only 225 square miles in area, the Island incorporates features reminiscent of various parts of the surrounding countries, ranging from high heather moorland, lush farmland and coastal heath.

The capital, Douglas, is situated on the east coast and is home to the Island's legislative buildings. Its financial services sector, a major part of the Island's economy, is also largely based here. To the south lies Castletown, overlooked by the imposing Castle Rushen and formerly the Island's capital and administrative centre. To the north is the town of Ramsey, while in the west lies Peel, a former fishing port and also dominated by a castle.

The Island has its own language, Manx Gaelic, which, though once in sharp decline, has undergone a resurgence in recent years. The Celtic inhabitants of the Island were never conquered by either the Romans or Anglo-Saxons, though the Norse raiders of the ninth century settled here in great numbers. They made the Island the centre of the Viking Kingdom of Mann and the Isles. Later the Isle of Man became a bargaining chip in the

Anglo-Scottish wars. Finally, it was purchased in 1765 by the crown from the Dukes of Atholl, by whom it had been inherited.

Today, the Island is perhaps best known for the tailless cat, and for the annual TT motorcycle races which are staged here each summer, but it is a place which will reward the curious traveller through the remarkable depth and richness of its culture and history.

CHAPTER 1

Celts and Vikings

The first humans arrived on the Isle of Man in the Mesolithic period, around 8000 BC. In the wake of the ice age, the Isle of Man was covered with deciduous woodland, dominated by oak and elm. Those first human settlers left no visible remains, and the main evidence for their presence comes from scatters of flint tools and the waste products from making these. They were hunter-gatherers and lived directly off their environment, following shoals of fish or perhaps hunting wild birds, and gathering naturally occurring fruit.

Over eighty early Mesolithic sites are now known from the Island. This relatively high density, when compared with Britain or Ireland, suggests that the Isle of Man was an important population centre at this time. Some evidence for the lifestyle of these people comes from the fact that a number of the sites are coastal, and some contain large quantities of shellfish, indicating a reliance upon the sea as a resource for food. Another significant characteristic is the presence of quantities of hazelnuts, which also provide good radiocarbon dating evidence.

Around 4000 BC the hunter-gatherer lifestyle changed into something quite different. From this era we begin to find the first evidence for farming and a more settled existence, in what is termed the Neolithic period. The earlier part of this era (c. 4000 to 3000 BC) is notable for the construction of a series of megalithic tombs, which provided a focus both for burial and for ritual activity. A number of these sites survive on the Isle of Man and can be visited. Perhaps the best example, and certainly the most studied is the **Meayll Circle** near Cregneash. It consists of six T-shaped burial chambers radiating from a central axis, and in many respects is unique in the British Isles. Other examples include **Cashtal yn Ard** and **King Orry's Grave**, and almost all of the Manx megalithic tombs occupy dominant locations with dramatic views of the horizon, sea and sky. During this era the Neolithic peoples undertook extensive clearance of the native woodlands of the Island

and had begun the process of turning it into an agricultural landscape such as we see today. The earliest evidence of a permanent dwelling on the Isle of Man was found at Ronaldsway during runway excavation work, and this house is also a strong contender for the oldest permanent inhabited structure in the British Isles. The area presently occupied by the Island's airport had long been recognised as also being, archaeologically, one of its most important sites.

During the later Neolithic period there is evidence to suggest that the people of the Isle of Man developed an identity quite distinct from that on either side of the Irish Sea. Much of this evidence, in the form of distinctively formed and decorated pottery, also comes from Ronaldsway, and the area gives its name to the so-called 'Ronaldsway culture'. During this period the disposal of the dead took place mainly through cremation, and archaeological evidence would suggest that the chambered tombs of the earlier period continued to provide a focus for this. The Manx Bronze age began around 2000 BC, when new metalworking technology began to appear on the Island. The earlier part of this era, lasting until roughly 1500 BC, is characterised by the construction of barrows or cairns, of which as many as 400 have been identified in the Manx landscape. However only a few of these have been properly investigated archaeologically. The general form consists of a stone cist or box, into which either the body or its cremated remains (often in a ceramic vessel) were placed. Grave goods such as bone pins, flint tools and metalwork could also be included. The cist was then covered with an earth mound or a cairn of stones. Sometimes standing stones or quartz boulders were used to define the perimeter of the cairn. A good example of this is the **Druid's Circle** at Orrisdale near Kirk Michael. Here a ring of stones form the edge of a burial mound, which antiquarian accounts record once contained a bronze age cremation urn. Today the mound presents a fairly low, overgrown appearance, having been partially eroded by farming activity in the nineteenth century. However, the presence of other mounds and stones in the vicinity – mostly now also altered or destroyed – suggests that this area may have had significance in prehistoric times as a funerary landscape. The name is misleading and seems to have been coined by Colonel Townley, an English diarist visiting the Isle of Man in the 1790s. At that time there was little understanding of prehistoric cultures, and any ancient monument was attributed to the Celts (the earliest inhabitants of the British Isles recorded in written sources) and their religious leaders, the Druids.

There are far fewer dramatic sites associated with the later Bronze Age. Perhaps the most significant is the hill fort and burial cairn on **South Barrule**, in the south of the Island. The cairn is located at the highest point on the hill, which is now marked by a modern Ordnance Survey triangulation pillar surrounded by an accompanying low wall. These modern features sit upon a low cairn comprised of tightly packed pieces of slate. The views from the summit are impressive, and the site was probably deliberately chosen, first, so that the dead could watch over the living, and second, to ensure that the monument was visible from most localities nearby, so that the living could see that they were being watched. Some time later a hill fort was constructed around it. This consists of a pair of roughly concentric earthworks, around 20 metres apart, surrounding the summit.

South Barrule, the most significant Bronze Age site on the Isle of Man

The outer rampart is the more impressive of the two, and is constructed largely of stone. This would have been transported up to the summit from the surrounding area, and also salvaged from the inner rampart (which must therefore be the earlier of the two). The outer rampart would originally have consisted of a stone wall several metres high, behind which a turf breastwork was constructed. There may also have been a ditch on the outside, indicating a considerable defensive feature. It was investigated by archaeologists in the 1970s, and a small area of excavated rampart has been left open in order to demonstrate the method of construction. The inner rampart once contained a collection of more than seventy roundhouses, of which one has been radiocarbon dated to around 500 BC – consistent with the late Bronze Age pottery found on the site. There has been much debate as to whether these structures were all inhabited, or whether some were storehouses for grain or livestock. Hill forts are generally considered to be responses to a threat from an external source; in the late Bronze Age there was certainly increasing competition for scarce resources, and evidence of warlike activity. For example, a skeleton from this era recovered from Ronaldsway was shown to have suffered a stab wound to his ribs inflicted with a bronze sword. Perhaps the fort was a means of protecting resources or people in times of threat. It may also have become the administrative centre or seat of power for the surrounding area. One of the principal archaeologists who investigated the South Barrule hill fort, Peter Gelling, wrote of it:

> It is legitimate ... to conclude that the fort was built by the native population of the Island, and is not necessarily an indication of invasion from outside. If so, it can still be asked why the fort was built at all. Perhaps one need only point to the quantities of very effective swords and spearheads which have come down to us from the late Bronze Age, and suggest that life was no more peaceful then than it was to be in the Iron Age. Yet one would have to admit that warfare is not considered to have been so endemic then as to induce people to live in so inhospitable a spot as the top of South Barrule.[1]

Interestingly, in Manx folklore South Barrule is held to be the seat of Manannan MacLir, the sea-god who protects the Isle of Man. Even into the eighteenth century, rushes gathered at the bottom of the hill were brought to the summit in tribute to him on Midsummer's Eve. Perhaps this was an echo of an earlier custom, in which tribute was made to a Bronze Age warlord or chieftain whose seat was within the fort.

From around 500 BC we begin to enter the Iron Age, though evidence for this period is somewhat sparse. Due to the acidic nature of Manx soils, few classic Iron Age objects survive, and sites from this era are rare. It is worth stating at this point that there was no Roman occupation of the Isle of Man. Though Roman coins have been found on the Island, their significance, and the degree of interaction between Roman Britain and the Isle of Man, remain matters of debate. The most significant landscape features from this period which survive today are a number of promontory forts, so named because an earth rampart and ditch close off a spit of land projecting out to sea, rather than encircling a hill top. A good example is **Burroo Ned**, overlooking the Sound, which is the largest such promontory fort on the Island. Here a collapsed embankment may be seen running roughly west-south-west to east-north-east, and this is all that survives of a once much more imposing structure, which may well have once been topped with a wooden fence or palisade. Inside the fort the remains of several roundhouses may sometimes be traced, especially in winter before the summer bracken obscures them. A field boundary to the north may follow the line of a second rampart. This and other promontory forts from this era, such as **Cass ny Hawin** and **Close ny Chollagh**, appear to have fallen out of use for several centuries, before being reoccupied during the Viking age.

During the Iron Age the people of the Isle of Man adopted Christianity, though the exact date and method by which this occurred are not clear. Some sources suggest links with the early Romano-British church, while there is also strong evidence for the influence of Irish Christianity associated with St Patrick. The structures most closely associated with this era are the keeills, small single-celled stone-built chapels, of which over 170 have been identified (of which around thirty-five exist in recognisable form above ground today). Very few have been investigated using modern archaeological means, so there are still many unanswered questions surrounding when they were constructed, how they were used, and indeed how they were roofed. The remote locations of many suggest an early form of Christianity in which priests or holy men lived as hermits, often under the patronage of local warlords and chieftains. The keeill which is believed to have existed on the Calf of Man would be a good example of this, and the spectacular Calf of Man crucifixion stone (one of the finest pieces of early Christian stonework in Europe) is believed to have been an altar frontal. It may be seen today in the **Manx Museum** in Douglas, along with numbers of other important carved stones. Two in particular carry an Ogham inscription and have been dated to the AD 600s. The similarities between these stones and those from the Irish midlands suggest settlement in (or at least contact with) that area. The presence of graves surrounding many keeill sites indicates that at least at certain times they had a communal role. Perhaps the best preserved example from the point of view of the visitor is **Lag ny Keeilley**. Here, the the site was extensively investigated in the early 1900s and revealed a rectangular stone structure (the keeill) enclosed within a roughly circular earth boundary. This is believed to represent the perimeter of the associated cemetery (or rhullick in Manx). A smaller stone structure has been interpreted as the priest's cell or dwelling, while an adjacent level area may have permitted him to grow crops. Again, the site is a remote and isolated location, though the absence of any finds which conclusively date the structures make it difficult to say a great deal with certainty about when and how they were used.

In the later years of the ninth century, Viking raiders in the Irish Sea began to settle upon the Isle of Man. Their presence is confirmed by a number of burials, found mostly in the north of the Island. These pagan graves contrast sharply with those of the Christian Manx population in this era, in that they contain grave goods for use in the afterlife. There are three main types: single burials under mounds, ship burials and burials within predominantly Christian cemeteries. The two ship burials are at Knock y Doonee in the north and at **Balladoole** in the south, while excavations in the Christian cemetery on St Patrick's Isle, Peel, in the 1980s revealed the grave of the 'Pagan Lady', a woman presumed to have been of high status and perhaps a healer. Buried with her were an iron rod, a pair of shears, a comb, a pestle and mortar, and a necklace of coloured glass, amber and jet, some parts of which would have been old even in her day, and which also suggested a wide range of trading links. Many of these items are on display in the **Manx Museum**.

Balladoole, the site of a dramatic viking ship burial, in a location which already had religious significance

The ship burial site at Balladoole is also accessible to visitors, at Chapel Hill west of Castletown. This area has been the focus of human activity since Mesolithic times, when hunter gatherers left evidence here. In the Iron Age a hill fort was constructed on the site, while in the Christian era a keeill and a cemetery were located here. When the boat-grave was constructed, it cut through the west-east orientated cist-graves and disturbed some of them, prompting debate regarding whether this is evidence of accommodation between Christian natives and incoming Norse elites, who respected the earlier religious use of the site, or alternatively the supplanting and deliberate slighting of the earlier graves, in order to impose the religion of the incomers onto a subjugated native population. What is known for certain, however, is that a clinker-built Viking ship of considerable size (estimated at 11 metres in length) was dragged up here from the shore. Within it was laid the body of a male, probably in his 30s, and alongside him were placed a variety of grave goods. Most spectacular of these was a set of horse harness and furniture. Other grave-goods included a shield boss, knives, strike-a-light and a whetstone. On top of the ship was placed a mound consisting of earth and cremated animal bone. This has been interpreted as the sacrifice of at least some of the Viking's livestock, and the topsoil from his fields, providing him with a living in the afterlife.

When it was excavated in the 1940s, all that remained of the ship was a complex pattern of the 300-or-so clench nails which had once held the timbers together. The positioning of stones on top of the mound also suggested that they had once supported the mast, protruding above ground and giving the site even greater prominence. Again, many of the more significant finds from this burial are displayed in the Manx Museum.

Also displayed here is the evidence for one of the most dramatic and controversial burials so far discovered from the Viking age Isle of Man, that at Ballateare. Here, as well as a heavily armed warrior, the grave also contained a female burial, the back of her head having been sliced off by a sword, and the possibility has been raised that she was a slave, also sacrificed in order to accompany her master into the next world.

In addition to the burials, around seventy carved or inscribed stone monuments are known from this period. Most are tenth century in date, and while many are Scandinavian in style, and depict scenes from Norse mythology, others display the influence of the native Manx population. Indeed some reflect both pagan and Christian beliefs, capturing the gradual Christianisation of the Vikings as they intermarried with, and were absorbed by, the native population. Another important consideration in relation to this is the fact that many were found at keeills, indicating a continuing religious function for these sites into the Viking era. Some of the best examples of Norse crosses are now to be found in Manx parish churches, where most were moved for safety around the end of the nineteenth century. The first curator of the Manx Museum, P.M.C. Kermode, did much to raise awareness of the importance of these carvings, many of which during his boyhood had been in use as horse tethering posts, lintels or plastered with bill posters in the centres of villages.

Gaut's Cross at Kirk Michael exhibits the 'ring chain' pattern which is common to many examples. It dates from AD 930–50, making it one of the earliest Viking carvings on the Isle of Man. Part of the inscription reads: 'Gaut made this, and all in Man'. This and the fact that his name also appears on another example at Andreas has led him to be regarded as the leading local carver of such works. Also important are Thorleif's Cross and Odd's Cross. These latter examples are to be found at **Old Kirk Braddan**, and although Christian they show a variety of dragons or other fantastical pagan beasts. Thorleif's cross also carries the runic inscription: 'Thorlief hnakki raised this cross in memory of Fiac, his son, Hafr's nephew.' Again in Old Kirk Braddan is a cross of the wheel-head type, which has been found in other parishes on the Island.

It is possible that further evidence of the fusion of Celtic and Norse cultures on the Isle of Man may come from the **Braaid**, an intriguing and well-preserved site in the south of the Island. Here two Norse longhouses from around AD 950 apparently coexisted alongside an earlier roundhouse, perhaps dating originally from AD 650.

It is rare to find source material from this era which allows us to connect known individuals with places on the Isle of Man, but in one particular case this might be possible. The thirteenth century *Njarl's Saga* describes events leading up to the Battle of Clontarf, near Dublin, in 1014. It speaks of two Viking brothers, Brodir and Ospak, of Danish descent, who lived on the west coast of the Isle of Man. The saga tells us:

> Brodir had been a Christian man and a mass-deacon by consecration, but he had thrown off his faith and become God's dastard, and now worshipped heathen fiends, and he was of all men most skilled in sorcery. He had that coat of mail on which no steel would bite. He was both tall and strong, and had such long locks that he tucked them under his belt. His hair was black.[2]

The two brothers were allied to King Sigtrygg, the Viking ruler of Dublin, and when war broke out between him and Brian Boru, High King of Ireland, they prepared fleets of ships. However, while his fleet was moored in the Sound, near the Calf of Man, Brodir's men were attacked by ravens. When Ospak learned of this, he took it as an omen that there would be much bloodshed, and defected to Brian Boru, becoming a Christian. Brodir, meanwhile, was killed at the ensuing battle.

The greatest legacy of the Vikings, however, is in the Manx system of parliamentary government, Tynwald, represented by **Tynwald Hill** at

Tynwald Hill, at St Johns. The site of political gatherings since Viking times (and possibly earlier), it is still the focal point for the Island's annual Tynwald Day ceremony

St John's. Wherever Vikings settled, from Iceland to Scandinavia and Russia, they would gather at least once a year to discuss laws and other matters. These sites often incorporate the Viking word 'thing' or 'thingvalla', meaning parliament site. It is known that other sites on the Island were used from time to time for Tynwald, and indeed it has been suggested that the Viking use of St Johns may simply be the continuation of a site which had been used for similar purpose by the native Manx, but in any case the location is supposed to represent the geographical centre of the Island, and legend has it that the hill incorporates turf from each of its parishes (though no archaeological work has ever been undertaken to verify this). The earliest written reference to an annual Manx Tynwald ceremony at St Johns dates from 1417 and it is considered to be the oldest continuous parliament in the world.

Each year on old Midsummer's Day, crowds still gather at St John's to hear the laws enacted in the previous twelve months read out in English and in Manx. This is a survival of Viking 'breast law' in which the legal code was not written down but carried in oral tradition, with the elders of the community able to recite them from the breast (or by heart, as we might say nowadays). Tynwald meets on the hill, and is sometimes presided over by the reigning monarch (as Lord of Mann) or they may be represented by a senior member of the royal family, or by the Lieutenant Governor. As the members of Tynwald process to the hill from the Chapel of St John, their path is strewn with rushes, an echo of the Celtic custom of offering rushes to the god Manannan on Midsummer's Eve. Participants also wear a sprig of 'bollan bane', or 'mugwort' as it is known in English. The herb was pre-eminent in Manx folk-medicine and white magic, and was believed to have the power to ward off evil. It has since been associated with the Christian festival of St John, which coincides with Tynwald Day. Once the members are seated, the First Deemster instructs the Coroner of Glenfaba to 'fence the court'. Again, this is an echo of a Viking custom in which the meeting would literally be surrounded by a palisade fence, and weapons would be left outside it – a precautionary measure in case disagreement should arise and violence break out. The lower house of Tynwald is known as the House of Keys, a name which is derived from the Manx term 'Yn Kiare as Feed', meaning 'the four and twenty,' as there are twenty-four members. During the era of the Norse kingdom the number included representatives from the Scottish Isles, until the loss of these territories to the Scottish crown. The **Tynwald Visitor Centre** at St John's contains information about 'thing sites' like Tynwald around the world, archive photos of the ceremony and the village, as well as details of other Manx calendar customs, how Tynwald works, and a Lego model of Tynwald Day. Younger visitors can choose from colouring-in, dressing up and building Lego to add to the model. There is more about Manx culture in the language and music room, as well as short films and books. A gift shop sells books and CDs relating to Manx history and culture, in particular Manx language and music.

The impact of the Vikings on the Isle of Man, and their fusion with the native Manx are among the themes explored at the **House of Manannan**, in Peel. This visitor centre also contains *Odin's Raven*, a ⅔ scale replica of the Gokstad ship, which was built in Norway and sailed from Trondheim to Peel, Isle of Man, by a joint Manx and Norwegian crew. The project formed part of the 1979 Manx Millennium Celebrations. The political legacy of the Norse in the form of Tynwald is also covered at the **Manx Museum** in Douglas, in the Viking and Medieval Gallery.

The most significant battle of this era was fought at Sky Hill, just outside Ramsey. Godred Crovan (known in Manx as King Orry) was a Norse descendant of one of the kings of Mann and the Isles. He spent some time at the Norwegian court, and was apparently part of Harald Hadrada's Viking army which was defeated at Stamford Bridge in 1066. From there he fled to the Isle of Man, where he was honourably received by the king (probably Godred II). When Godred II died in 1075, the throne passed to his son, Fingall, but he does not seem to have retained it for long. In 1075, Godred Crovan assembled a fleet and an army, probably of Norsemen from the Hebrides, and attacked the Island. He was repulsed, but was soon back for a second attempt. Again he was repulsed, but it is during this period that Fingall 'disappears' from the record, and it is probable he was killed during one of the invasion attempts. In 1079, Godred Crovan came back, and the Chronicles of Mann are reasonably clear as to what happened next:

> A third time he gathered a massive force and came by night to the harbour which is called Ramsey, and three hundred men he hid in a wood which was on the sloping brow of the mountain called Sky Hill. At dawn the Manxmen formed up in battle order and after a massive charge joined battle with Godred. When the battle was raging vehemently, the three hundred rose from their place of hiding at their rear and began to weaken the resistance of the Manxmen and compelled them to flee. Now when they saw themselves defeated without any place for them to escape to, for the tide had filled the riverbed at Ramsey and the enemy were pressing constantly from the other side, those that were left begged Godred with pitiful cries to spare them their lives. Moved with compassion and taking pity on their plight, since he had been reared among them for some time, he called off his army and forbade them to pursue them further.[3]

A monument commemorating the Battle of Sky Hill, in 1079

After the battle of Sky Hill in 1079 the Chronicle states that:

Godred then granted to the few islanders who had remained with him, the southern part of the island, and to the surviving Manxmen the northern portion.[4]

The dividing line was not the central valley running between Douglas and Peel but rather the mountain range running diagonally along the spine of the Island. This would remain a feature of Manx culture for many years to come, and led to the creation of two parallel administrations each of which has its Castle, Deemster, and Vicar-General. Although there is no direct archaeological evidence for the site of the battle, a monument to it may be found not far from **Milntown House**. More solid archaeological evidence for the uncertainty of these times comes from the numerous coin hoards from this era which have been discovered on the Island. Many of these are now on display in the Manx Museum in Douglas.

Viewed another way, however, the hoards are evidence of rising prosperity in the eleventh century. Almost as much Viking silver has been found on the Isle of Man as from the whole of Ireland. Although these hoards are traditionally viewed as booty from violent raids against unprotected English monasteries, numbers of the coins found come from the reign of the Anglo-Saxon King Edgar, and are most likely the product of trade instead. The Isle of Man was certainly a centre of high quality metalwork at this time. Fragments of jewellery found in the Castle Esplanade hoard from Chester may well have been made on the Isle of Man, and the Anglo-Saxon coins may be evidence of commerce as much as anything else. The important Viking grave at Knock-Y-Doonee, Andreas contained the tools of a blacksmith – hammer, tongs and a cauldron, and one of Gaut's crosses records that the man who commissioned it was 'the son of Athakan the Smith'.

Environmental evidence also indicates there was a period of climatic warming across northern Europe in this period. Winters were milder, and the growing season longer. The Viking age farm at Dooarlish Cashen, dating from around AD 1000 was built on marginal land, previously unsuitable for agriculture (as it would become once more in the modern era). More capacity for food production meant that there was a surplus left over for trade once the immediate needs of the farmer's family had been met. All this contributed to the growing prosperity of the Island. However, its survival as an independent Norse kingdom would look increasingly precarious in the centuries which followed, particularly as its neighbours and rivals England and Scotland grew in power.

CHAPTER 2

The Middle Ages

By the end of the eleventh century, the Viking chieftain Godred Crovan (sometimes identified as a survivor of Harald Hadrada's Norse army which was defeated at Stamford Bridge in 1066, and known in Manx as King Orry) had established himself on the Isle of Man. Having driven off his rivals on the Island, Crovan's Kingdom of Mann and the Isles would survive until 1266, when the Isle of Man passed to the King of Scotland under the terms of the treaty of Perth. The two main administrative centres of Peel Castle and Castle Rushen began to develop during this era. Peel Castle also had a religious function, which was further strengthened by ecclesiastical reorganisations at this time. The other important aspect of medieval religious life was monasticism, and on the Isle of Man Rushen Abbey, the Nunnery at Douglas and Bemaken Friary at Ballabeg all developed alongside it.

These times were characterised by internecine warfare and in 1098 a battle was fought at a place named **Santwat** in what seems to have been a Manx civil war, between those from the north and their counterparts in the south. The exact location of this battle is disputed, as are the origins of the two sides. Their respective leaders, Earls Ottar and Macmaras, both fell in the conflict. Their names, one of Norwegian origin and the other Celtic, have led to speculation that this was a contest between the descendants of Crovan, and the survivors of the original Manx population. Manx folklore has it that the men of the south were victorious because their womenfolk came to their aid at a key moment in the fighting, carrying rocks and stones to hurl at the enemy. A further intriguing reference to this conflict comes from the Chronicles of Mann and the Isles, which states that later the same year King Magnus Barefoot (or Magnus Barelegs) of Norway landed at St Patrick's Isle and went to view the site of the battle, where many bodies still lay unburied.

It has been speculated that the obvious place for the fighting to have taken place would have been on the dividing line between the two provinces, and in former times local folklore had it that the site was in fact near Peel. The bridge on the St John's to Patrick road is still called 'the bridge of the bloody battle'. Nearby is Glen Craue, in Manx 'the Glen of Bones'. This would tally with bodies lying unburied for some time. The Chronicles state that the conflict left the Island so weakened that afterwards it fell easily to Magnus Barefoot. However within a generation the descendants of Godred Crovan had reasserted control over the kingdom.

When Magnus landed at St Patrick's Isle, he would probably have found what would become Peel Castle, consisting at that time mainly of a wooden stockade fence. Its natural defensive features have always made it an attractive location, indeed until relatively recently, with the construction of the causeway, St Patrick's Isle was only accessible from Peel at low tide. Although the site has been in use since prehistoric times, and in the Bronze Age it was occupied by a number of roundhouses, in the early Christian

St Patrick's Isle and Peel Castle, seen in the early years of the Twentieth Century (Library of Congress)

era it was the location of just some religious buildings and a cemetery. Indeed the earliest stone structures on the islet were religious in nature, being St Patrick's church, St Patrick's chapel and the Round Tower. Towers such as this are commonly found at monastic sites in Ireland from about AD 800 to 1100, and reflect the troubled nature of those times. They provided a refuge for the monastic community from raiders, in particular Norsemen.

The arrival of the Viking dynasty under Magnus coincided with a shift in purpose at St Patrick's Isle away from a mainly religious function towards one combining ecclesiastical and military duties. The Chronicles of Mann suggest that St German's cathedral was constructed by Simon, Bishop of Sodor, in about 1257, and although the church was nominally in control of the islet, its dual military and religious role was the source of some tension. The defensive structures which are currently visible were begun in the late 1300s, and to start with this involved the construction of a number of freestanding stone towers, the earliest of which is probably the gatehouse. Initially these may have been connected by an earth rampart, but this was later replaced by a stone curtain wall, along with additional towers. Evidence for this sequence comes from the fact that the earlier towers sit somewhat awkwardly on the later wall circuit, and do not always provide such effective flanking fire as the purpose-built towers.

In tandem with Peel Castle, Castle Rushen began to develop as the administrative centre of the Island and the seat of the kings of Mann and the Isles. It may have been founded by Norse King Magnus Barefoot, who it is recorded constructed three forts on the Isle of Man; the others being Peel Castle, and perhaps the **Broogh Fort** at Santon. The name of this latter feature is derived from the Manx word meaning a steep slope or cliff, and aptly describes the artificially steep sides of the mound, which is the chief characteristic of this site. The mound is only about 3 metres higher than the surrounding ground level, and its flat top is about 20 metres across. It is surrounded by a ditch and bank which are most obvious on the south-east side, and which have been destroyed by the road to the south-west. Waterlogged ground to the north ensures that the base of the ditch is always wet. The site has never been investigated; no evidence has been found to show what may have been constructed on top of the artificial mound, and no artefacts have been found which might answer the question of its age.

Another contender for one of Mangus's three forts is **Cronk Howe Mooar** near Port Erin. We now know that this rather unassuming hillock is in fact a classic motte and bailey castle. It has all the elements of a type of defensive structure introduced by the Normans when they invaded England in 1066. It has an artificial hill with a moat around it, a ramp coming to the edge of the moat where there would have been a drawbridge, and an area beyond, on the flat ground, where a paling fence would have protected people and buildings, and maybe livestock as well. The pit on the top was actually the base for the castle that once stood there, probably made of wood. Archaeological investigation has revealed that the mound was made in layers. This was a technique developed by the Normans to give greater stability to these artificial hills. A single pile of soil would be likely to erode or eventually wash away. However, the layering strengthened the structure, and large timbers were often included for added durability.

As Castle Rushen developed, its form was certainly influenced by that of the Norman castles being built across England and Wales at this time, and it was clearly intended both as a statement of power in the landscape, and as an imposing 'front door' to the kingdom, as the first sight met with by visiting dignitaries or ambassadors from other realms. One of the earliest references to it is to be found in the Chronicles of Mann, where it is stated that King Magnus Olafson died there in 1265. However, the oldest parts of the stonework, the lower courses of the central keep, probably date to the reign of Reginald (1187–1226). Following the death of Magnus, the Isle of Man became a pawn in the Anglo-Scottish wars. Robert the Bruce laid siege to the castle in 1313, and extensive rebuilding work in the wake of this event might suggest that considerable damage was inflicted. With the English firmly back in control by the 1330s, major work on the castle continued. This included raising the height of the keep and remodelling the front wall, as well as constructing a new east tower.

When considering Castle Rushen it is also important to bear in mind **Rushen Abbey**, at nearby Ballasalla. The Chronicles of Mann record that in 1134 King Olaf granted land to the Abbot of Furness in Cumbria to establish a monastery on the Isle of Man. This grew into a thriving community, as evidenced by the large number of burials recorded from around the site. As well as the monks themselves, there were lay brothers who helped with

THE MIDDLE AGES 19

Castle Rushen, overlooking Castletown Harbour. As the 'gateway' to the Kingdom of Mann, construction began in the Norse era

labour, and tenant farmers who rented lands around the abbey. If Castle Rushen represented earthly power, then Rushen Abbey was the seat of the Norse kings' spiritual authority, the two linked in the landscape by the Silverburn river.

In the twelfth century the **chapel of St Michael** was constructed on a small islet in Derbyhaven (only in the eighteenth century was it connected to Langness by a causeway). The chapel is built of limestone blocks, with three internal cells and a bell cote at one end. Originally it would have had a slate roof. A number of medieval cist burials have been discovered around the chapel and it continued as a burial place for shipwrecked mariners and for Catholics until the nineteenth century.

There are strong indications that the now ruined chapel of **St Trinians**, standing on the north side of the main road from Douglas to Peel, is also from the twelfth century. The name Trinian is one of many forms of Ninian, and it is believed that the first structure on this site was established during the reign of Olaf I (1103–1155). However, sources indicate that it was further developed as a 'hospital' or sanctuary for the poor in the time of Godred II. He married Phingola, daughter of MacLoughlin, a son of the great Murkartac O'Loughlin, King of Ulster, and Monarch of Ireland. This Irish princess belonged to a family associated with the endowment of religion, and her marriage took place in 1177, at a period when the 'hospital' as an institution to be established and endowed had a vogue in Ireland. Cardinal Vivian, the Papal Legate, was present in Man at Phingola's marriage, accompanied by Silvanus, Abbot of Rievaulx, who performed the marriage ceremony. That the building was originally a hospital or hospice for the poor is supported by the fact that it stands in the great gap in the hills and exactly on the divide of the Island, between the north-western and south-eastern regions, beside a highroad which was doubtless a travel route much earlier than the twelfth century. It was dissolved in 1587 as part of the Scottish reformation, when its properties were vested in the King of Scots. It is a curious fact that for centuries, until the decline of the Manx language, St Trinian's was called by the country people: 'the broken Church', a name or an expression that may have originated in an act of breaking or removing the roof. Indeed, to the regret of later archaeologists, much material, including some mouldings, was removed from St Trinian's in 1780 and conveyed to the old parish church of Marown, where it was used in the rebuilding of the western gable and doorway, and the porch which formed a series of steps to reach the door to the western gallery.

Later Manx folklore attributes the missing roof to the legend of the Buggane, a monstrous creature which inhabited the hills around Greeba and which took exception to the construction of the church. Sophia Morrison, writing in *Manx Fairy Tales*, tells us:

> So when the roof of the church was first put on, there was heard that very night a dreadful sound in it, and when the people of Greeba got up early next morning they found their church roofless, and planks and broken beams all around the place. After a time, and with great effort, the roof was put on again. But when it was on, a great storm arose in the night and it was blown down from the walls, exactly as had happened before. This fall put fear in the people, for they were sure now that it was the evil, destructive Buggane himself that was doing the mischief. But, though they were terrified, they resolved to make one more attempt; and the third roof was nearly finished.[5]

Only one brave soul, a tailor from Greeba, dared to defy the Buggane, and wagered that he would make a pair of breeches there. The monstrous creature tried to terrify the tailor but:

> Before he could utter another syllable, or pull the other foot out of the ground, the little Tailor quickly jumped up, and made two stitches together. The breeches were at last finished, then with one spring he made a leap through the nearest window. But scarcely was he outside the walls when down fell the new roof with a terrible crash, that made Tim jump a great deal more nimbly than he ever did before. Hearing the Buggane's fiendish guffaws of laughter behind him, he took to his heels and sped hot-foot along the Douglas road, the breeches under his arms and the furious Buggane in full chase. The Tailor made for Marown Church, only a little distance away, and knew he would be safe if he could only reach the churchyard. He ran faster still, he reached the wall, he leaped over it like a hunted hare, and fell weary and spent upon the grass, under the shadow of the church, where the Buggane had not power to follow.

> So furious was the monster at this that he seized his own head with his two hands, tore it off his body and sent it flying over the wall after the Tailor. It burst at his feet with a terrific explosion, and with that the Buggane vanished, and was never seen or heard of afterwards. Wonderful to relate, the Tailor was not hurt, and he won the wager, for no person grumbled at the few long stitches put into the breeches.[6]

In due course, Rushen Abbey gave rise to the **Old Grammar School** in Castletown, originally the chapel of St Mary, which was constructed by the monks as a chapel of ease to serve the community growing up around the castle. It is believed to date from the early 1200s, and the lowest courses of masonry are built directly on to the bedrock. The building had a dual function as a chapel and the town schoolroom until 1702, when a new St Mary's church was constructed in Castletown square. From then on the building served only as a school until it closed in 1930. It is often referred to as the oldest roofed building in the Isle of Man.

In 1266, with Norwegian influence weakening throughout the Scottish Islands, King Alexander III of Scotland secured control of the Isle of Man by means of the Treaty of Perth. Although he sent a number of his bailiffs to administer the Island on his behalf, the Manx were soon in revolt against Scottish rule. In 1275, Godred Magnusson, an illegitimate son of Magnús Óláfsson, King of Mann and the Isles, ejected the Scottish overlords and took control of the Island's fortifications. Alexander III quickly responded by sending an army drawn from territories loyal to him to invade the island and restore Scottish royal authority. The Scottish force appears to have been composed of a small component of heavily armed knights, a contingent of infantry troops levied from the common army of Galloway, and a fleet of galleys gathered from the Hebrides, and it was more than a match for its Manx opponents.

The Scots made landfall on the southern shores of Mann, and according to the Chronicle of Lanercost and the Chronicles of Mann, the invaders first attempted to resolve the uprising peaceably, demanding that the rebels stand down and submit to Alexander III. That was not to be, and the ensuing Battle of Ronaldsway saw the Manx heavily defeated. The account preserved in the sources suggests that the lightly armed and poorly trained rebels were soundly crushed by well-armed Scottish warriors, with the Annals of Lanercost declaring that 'the wretched Manxmen turned their backs, and perished miserably'. Although the Chronicles of Mann specifies that 537 people were slaughtered by the Scots, it is possible that this tally owes itself to contemporary poetic convention, as the source further quotes the following rhyming lament: 'ten times fifty, three times ten and five and two did fall; O Manx race, beware lest future catastrophe you befall'.

Upon the successful subjugation of the Manx, Alexander III installed his son, also called Alexander, as Lord of Mann. Although this 11-year-old child was too young to govern in person, his elevation to the lordship reinforced Scottish control of the Island. The bestowal of Mann as a royal appanage openly designated the prince as the heir to the Scottish throne, and enabled the authority of the Scottish crown to be personally represented on Manx soil. Evidence of further trouble faced by the Scots on Mann occurs in 1288, when the Sheriff of Dumfries rendered an account for the expense of guarding the lands of a person slain on the island in the service of the Scottish king. As it turned out, Scottish control was not long-lasting, and before the end of the century the Manx placed themselves under the overlordship of the English crown.

A postscript to this battle comes in the form of the 1936 expansion of Ronaldsway airport. Workmen excavating a series of mounds uncovered a mass grave, with the bones of many men apparently thrown in in disorder. It was assumed that these were the casualties of the battle in 1275. During the 1270s we also find the earliest references to the Three Legs of Man in use as a device to represent the Kingdom of Mann. Segar's Roll of around 1280 provides an illustration of three legs in chain mail, running clockwise, joined at a triangle. Some of the Scottish warlords who came to the Island under Bruce used the device as part of their heraldry, though it is not clear if they brought it with them, or took it away when they left.

Later during the Anglo-Scottish wars, Edward III had granted the Island and the title of King of Mann to William Montacute, 1st Earl of Salisbury, in a document which read:

> The whole right and claim that We have, We have had, or in any manner shall We be able to have in the future, in the island of Man with all its privileges, so that neither We, nor Our heirs, or any other in Our name, will not demand or avenge in the future the aforesaid right or claim to the island.[7]

The Island continued to be held by this family until William Le Scrope, Earl of Wiltshire, was executed for treason by Henry IV. The Kingdom of Mann then passed briefly to Henry Percy, Earl of Northumberland, before he too was executed. In 1405 Henry IV granted the Isle of Man to Sir John Stanley, thus beginning a long association between the Island and the Stanley family. They would assume the title King of Mann, though with homage and tribute of two falcons due to each King of England upon his coronation. Over the next 300 years the Stanleys created in the Isle of Man a unique legal and administrative framework, which is unparalleled either by those in England or Scotland. This is at one level reflected by the many offices of state which have no direct equivalent in the United Kingdom, and the unique titles such as Deemster which are found in the Isle of Man. Sir John's son, John II, was a rare visitor to the Island, coming only twice in order to put down rebellions, but he did much to codify Manx law by having it set down in writing. The historian A.W. Moore said of him:

> He may justly be considered an enlightened and upright ruler, much in advance of his time. He caused the ancient laws and constitutions of his little kingdom to be reduced to writing, he humbled the overbearing ecclesiastical authorities, and, after he had practically concentrated all power into his own hands, he wisely conceded a representative form of government.[8]

In 1485, in recognition of his support for Henry Tudor at the Battle of Bosworth, Sir Thomas Stanley was given the title of Earl of Derby. The Earls of Derby would hold the title of King (later Lord) of Mann until 1736, when it passed to the Atholl family, but it would be their influence which would shape the structures and form of Manx law and administration which have survived into the modern era.

CHAPTER 3

The Civil War Era and Eighteenth Century

By the early 1500s the Kingship of Mann had passed to Sir Thomas Stanley. He later renounced the title, in favour of that of Lord of Man, stating that he would rather be a great lord than a petty king. His decision was no doubt influenced by the jealousy of Henry VIII, who would not long have tolerated a rival king within his realm. Among other things the Stanleys improved and expanded Castle Rushen, adding a glacis to the ramparts around 1540 in order to increase its resistance to the new technology of cannon and gunpowder. The Lord's apartments in the castle were also finely decorated in this era.

The height of Stanley influence came in the era of the 7th Earl, James Stanley, known to the Manx as Yn Stanlagh Mooar (the great Stanley). James was a loyal follower of Charles I, and during the Civil War placed all of his possessions at the king's disposal. During this time Castle Rushen became a Royalist court in exile, the Stanleys holding masked balls and entertaining those members of

James Stanley, 7th Earl of Derby. Lord of Mann in the 1640s, he held the Island for the King

the aristocracy who had been forced to flee England. James Stanley expended much effort during the Civil War in improving the defences of the Isle of Man. He rearmed the Tudor-era forts at Douglas and on St Michael's Isle, covering Derbyhaven. He improved the defences of Peel Castle by adding loopholes for musketeers, while at Castle Rushen he enlarged and improved the domestic accommodation; in addition he constructed an entirely new earthwork at **Kerroogarrow (Ballachurry)**, in the north of the Island. The fort is star shaped with bastions at each corner allowing covering fire along the walls, which were probably topped with a wooden palisade in the seventeenth century. The remote location of the fort has long puzzled historians, and exactly what it was intended to protect remains a mystery. Some claim that it was used for training purposes; another theory has it that the northern plain was much wetter in those days, and so any army landing at Ramsey and wishing to attack Peel would have to follow the high ground leading past this fort.

Kerroogarrow Fort, built by Stanley as part of his programme of improving the Island's defences. © Isle of Man Government Cartographic Office

Stanley also appropriated the bishop's residence, **Bishopscourt**, following the death of the incumbent in 1643. Between 1648 and 1651 the earl constructed a substantial earthen ditch and rampart around the tower house, with a bastion at each corner, effectively creating a rectangular fort. Part of these defences can still be seen to the north-east of Bishopscourt. Following the eventual capture and execution of Charles I, James Stanley was despondent; yet when Cromwell offered him amnesty and the return of half of his estates for his surrender, he was enraged. His famous reply ran as follows:

> Sir, I received your letter with indignation and scorn, and return you this answer, that I cannot but wonder whence you should gather any hopes from me that I should, like you, prove treacherous to my Sovereign, since you cannot but be sensible of my former actings in his late Majesty's service; from which principles of Loyalty I am in no whit departed. I scorn your proffers, disdain your favour and abhor your treason, and am so far from delivering up this Island to your advantage, that I will keep it to the utmost of my power and your destruction. Take this for your final answer and forbear any further solicitations; for if you trouble me with any more messages on this occasion, I will burn the paper and hang the bearer. This is the immutable resolution and shall be the undoubted practice of him who accounts it his chiefest glory to be,
>
> His Majesty's most Loyal and obedient Servant, DERBY.[9]

Hearing of the return of Charles II, Stanley raised an army in the Isle of Man and travelled to Lancashire to fight for him. The campaign ended disastrously, with Charles II forced into exile and Stanley captured. After a sham trial on trumped-up charges, he was executed at Bolton by Parliamentary forces. Now Parliament decided to crush the resistance of the Island once and for all. A fleet arrived in Ramsey Bay, under the command of Colonel Robert Duckenfield. In the meantime, a domestic rebellion against the Stanleys had broken out, under the leadership of the powerful Christian family. The issue of land tenure had long been contentious, with James Stanley attempting to remove the right of Manx families to hold the lease on land over successive generations. William Christian (known in Manx as Illiam Dhone, or brown haired William) the commander of the

Island's militia and once James Stanley's closest ally, hoped that he could secure these rights through negotiating the surrender of the Island to the Parliamentary forces. His actions have been seen variously as a betrayal of the Duchess, Charlotte de Tremoille, who commanded the Island's defences in her husband's absence, or as the act of a Manx patriot, defending the interests of his people. He remains to this day an iconic figure in the Manx nationalist movement.

When Illiam Dhone's men arrived at Kerroogarrow on 21 October 1651 to take over, the fort was garrisoned, and there were heated exchanges at the gate. The commander of the fort, Major Thomas Stanley, refused to cooperate. Outside William Teare and Ewan Curghey were shouting at him about the duplicity of Lady Derby and her own secret negotiations with the Parliamentary forces. Ewan Curghey, enraged that the fort held out, sent one of his soldiers off into the nearby countryside to set fire to the property of John McSayle, a soldier of the garrison. When the flames were seen rising in the distance the men inside started to desert and the fort was quickly taken. It was to surrender to the Parliamentary forces in Ramsey five days later. The two castles likewise were surrendered without a fight.

Some years later, with the restoration of the monarchy, Charles Stanley the 8th Earl returned to the Island to reclaim his property. The terms of the restoration had expressly forbidden acts of retribution for incidents during the Civil War, but Stanley did not believe that this applied on the Isle of Man. He had Illiam Dhone put on trial for treason, and he was condemned to death. His supporters appealed directly to Charles II, and a letter of pardon from the king himself arrived on the Isle of Man just too late to prevent Illiam Dhone's execution by firing squad at **Hango Hill** (now considered a shrine to the martyr, and the site of a gathering by Manx nationalists each year on the anniversary). Charles Stanley was later summoned to London, for a dressing down by the furious Charles II. Interestingly, the area around Hango Hill had traditionally been used by the Derby family as the site of a horse race, for the purpose of encouraging the improvement of Manx horse stock, and the 7th Earl had even given a trophy as a prize. This is believed to be the oldest horse racing event in the British Isles. Known as the 'Manx Derby' it was the forerunner of the Derby now held at Epsom. The historic home of the Christian family, **Milntown** near Ramsey, is occasionally open during the summer for guided tours, though little remains from the seventeenth century beyond the fabric of the building.

Following the Civil War, the Isle of Man largely avoided the frenzy of witch hunting which overtook much of England and Scotland. Only one Manx woman is recorded as having been put to death for witchcraft, Margaret Inequane in 1617. She was burned at the stake near Castletown market cross, and her death so horrified the Manx population that they were reluctant to convict anyone for witchcraft thereafter. However, the survival of pre-Christian beliefs in the remoter parts of the Isle of Man is not wholly surprising. What is rather more intriguing is the leniency with which the Manx ecclesiastical courts usually treated it. A transcript of a typical case, along with the penalties imposed, is given below:

> Bishop's Court, 30th September, 1659 – Whereas Mrs Jane Cesar hath been accused upon suspicion of witchcraft, charminge or sorscerie, where upon certaine examinacons have been taken. And the said case being putt to the triall of a jurie, they the said jurors (after examinacon of the business) have this day cleared and acquitted ye said Jane Cesar of the accusacon aforesaid as by theire Answere may appeare. Nevertheles that the said Jane Cesar may declare her inocencie of such practizes and that shee doth renounce the same as diabolicall and wicked; she is hereby ordered to acknowledge the same before the Congregacon off [sic] Kk. Malew Parish on the next Lord's day to the end that others may be admonished to relinquish detest and abhor such delusions which are of great inducement to greater temptacons and are too frequently practised in this Island as is dayly observed. Of which if any one shalt be hereafter accused and the same lawfully proved such persons are to be severely fined and punished, or otherwise proceeded against accordinge as the law doth provide in such cases. (Signed) Jam. Chaloner.
>
> To Sr. Tho. Parr minister of Kk Malew who is to read ye before his Congregacon the next Sabbath in English and Manxe and to return this Order with the acknowledgment made as aforesaid into the Comptrouleres office afterwards. True Coppie agreeinge with ye originall.
>
> October the 2th, 1659 (Signed) J. Woods.[10]

As the eighteenth century opened, the Isle of Man was riding the crest of a new wave of prosperity. This came as a result of the lower rate of import duty imposed by the Derby family, and their successors the Dukes of Atholl, who inherited the Island in 1736. This differential in taxes encouraged merchants to land their goods – brandy, rum, spices, tea and other luxury items – in the Isle of Man, rather than at the harbours of the United Kingdom. Much of it, however, was then illicitly re-exported to those shores under cover of darkness. To the officers of the British customs and excise this was smuggling, plain and simple, but the Manx authorities maintained that it was no concern of theirs, and that no illegality had occurred from their point of view. Thus the 'running trade' as it was known, became the staple legitimate commerce of the Island for the best part of sixty years. Great fortunes were made, and businessmen came to live on the Island from many parts of Europe. It was said that many of the buildings in Douglas greatly resembled those of Antwerp or other Flemish ports, though much of this architecture has now sadly gone. Only the Adam doorway at the lower entrance to the **Manx Museum** site, which was saved from a demolished property in the 1930s, now offers a reminder of the opulence of some of the buildings of this era.

This situation could not last, however, and finally the British government decided to close the loophole by purchasing the regalities of the Island from the Duke of Atholl. By this stage it was estimated that the British exchequer was losing an astonishing £300,000 a year through the Isle of Man, and in 1765 the Act of Revestment was passed, returning control of the Island to the crown. Many of the merchants subsequently sold up and left, their fine houses by the harbour later being divided up for use as slum tenements. Not surprisingly it took some time to completely stamp out the illicit import and export of sprits and tobacco, and many isolated coves and inlets have smuggling stories associated with them. Frequently these places also have tales from Manx folklore connected with them, as rumours of supernatural beings were useful as a means of keeping away prying and unwanted eyes. Equally well, strange lights visible at night could easily be explained as 'themselves', or fairies. Perhaps the most evocative of these smuggling sites is **Niarbyl**, and it too comes with a story, that of the 'fairy coopers', who could be heard hammering casks in the nearby caves late at night.

THE CIVIL WAR ERA AND EIGHTEENTH CENTURY

Following the Act of Revestment, the British government exercised its new authority over the Island through the office of Governor (a position which had previously existed during the Atholl rule, as the duke could not be present on the Island at all times). However, the 4th Duke of Atholl, who believed that his father had been short changed in the purchase of the Island, constantly petitioned the Westminster parliament for a review of the terms of the Act of Revestment. As part of a package intended to placate him in this, he was appointed to the role of Governor of the Isle of Man. This was something of a sinecure, and like his predecessors, he was away so much that it became necessary to create the post of Lieutenant Governor to assist him. After his demise, the post of Governor lapsed, and today only the office of Lieutenant Governor survives.

Another consequence of the acquisition of the Island by the British government was that Douglas became an important base for the Royal Navy. Its vessels regularly put into port here for repairs and supplies while on coastal patrol service in the Irish Sea, and a number of the officers had homes or settled on the Island. Among them were several who had sailed with Captain Cook on his journeys of exploration in the Pacific, notably Peter Fannin, Benjamin Bechino, and a young man hoping to climb the naval career ladder by the name of William Bligh. He came to the Island in the 1770s, and fell in love with the daughter of the Island's tax inspector. The two were married in Onchan, and spent the early part of their married life in lodgings in Douglas. At least one of their daughters was baptised at St Matthew's church, on Douglas harbourside. It was while they were living in Douglas that Bligh was introduced to a young man from a

Lieutenant William Bligh RN, of Bounty fame, who resided on the Isle of Man in the early 1780s

respectable family, but one which had fallen on hard times. That young man, Fletcher Christian, also wished to make a career in the navy, but for the time being the two sailed together on merchant ships to the West Indies. A friendship developed between them, and when in 1788 Bligh was offered the chance to command an expedition to collect breadfruit seedlings to feed the slaves on the West Indian plantations, he naturally took Christian with him. The ship they sailed on was HMS *Bounty*, and the mutiny which followed is possibly one of the the most famous events in British naval history. It has been the subject of three Hollywood films, and countless books and articles. Few people today, however, are aware of the fact that Douglas was the cradle of these events, perhaps because so little remains of the town which Bligh and Christian would have known. There are however a few echoes still to be found.

Perhaps the best place to start is at **St George's Church** in Douglas. At the time Christian and Bligh lived here, the church was newly built and stood on its own in a field on the edge of the little town. It is almost certainly here that the seeds of the *Bounty* mutiny were sown, for it was at this church that Bligh's father-in-law Richard Bethem, Captain John Taubman (who was related by marriage to the Christians) and Peter John Heywood worshipped. Heywood was a Douglas gentleman, formerly the agent for the Duke of Atholl, and had fallen on hard times. Bethem, anxious to help him, persuaded Bligh to take his son Peter Heywood as a midshipman aboard the *Bounty*. Taubman meanwhile had probably played a part in introducing Bligh to Fletcher Christian. As the *Bounty*'s mission took her to Tahiti in 1788, a close bond would grow up between Christian and Heywood, both young men from a well-to-do family who now had nothing but their family name. This made Bligh deeply suspicious, and when Christian eventually turned against him, he famously declared that he regretted the day he ever saw a Manxman, a Christian or a Heywood.

In the heart of Douglas itself, most of the eighteenth century buildings have gone, but on North Quay the **Douglas Hotel** survives. This impressive five bayed four storey house was built in 1758 by an Irish merchant named Black, and it serves to underline the prosperity of the town in the years of the running trade. In the panic that followed the Act of Revestment it was sold off, and was one of the properties which the canny Duke was able to snap up

The Douglas Hotel, once the home of Peter Heywood, who was sentenced to death for his part in the Mutiny on the Bounty

at a bargain price. He allocated it to his Seneschal Peter John Heywood, and it thus became the home of the young Peter Heywood. A five minute walk takes us to **Fort Street**, and a modern bakery now stands on the approximate site of Fletcher Christian's home.

Interestingly, Fletcher's younger brother Humphrey, who would also have grown up in this house, became the mate aboard a slave ship and died when it exploded at Bonny, in West Africa. As gunpowder was frequently traded for slaves, such explosions were not uncommon. Humphrey was not the only Manx crewman to become involved in this cruellest of trades. Many of the Liverpool slave ships were crewed by Manxmen, and indeed it was said that some of the most successful captains there were Manx. One of the most important surviving testimonies concerning the transatlantic slave trade was penned by a Ramsey man, Hugh Crow, who made his living as the captain of a number of such ships. Indeed, he made what is believed to have been the last legal British slave journey aboard the ship *Kitty's Amelia*, just as abolition came into effect. Many of the warehouses of Douglas held 'Guinea Goods', trinkets and other items to be bartered in West Africa, and it was common for a slave ship to stop here to collect these items before setting sail. We know a great deal about the crewmen aboard such ships, and the dangers which they faced from Yellow Fever and other tropical diseases, from the many sailors' wills held in the archives of the **Manx Museum**. We also know a great deal about the merchants who based themselves in Douglas at this time. Several it seems had a black slave as a personal servant, as was fashionable at the time. The grand doorways of some of the houses which survive near the harbour are also echoes of this time.

Further along the sea front can be found the **Castle Mona**, which was built by the 4th Duke of Atholl as his Manx residence. The duke had previously lived at two properties near the harbour but found neither to his liking. Instead he opted to build a new home, and imported both the stone and the architect (George Steuart) from Scotland for the purpose. The only other structure on the Isle of Man made from this type of Arran stone is the memorial to his brother, Lord Henry Murray (also designed by Steuart), which can be found in Old Kirk Braddan churchyard. Castle Mona was completed in 1804 and once stood in splendid isolation on this part of the shore. The encroachment of other buildings in the 200 years or more since it was completed have left it much less visually imposing than it once was, though there were those even at the time of construction who found it unimpressive. Hannah Bullock, writing in 1816, stated:

> The Duke of Atholl's house or castle, as it is the first object which strikes the eye of the traveller, and the most considerable for magnitude in the island, must not be passed over with the slight notice already taken of it. It is an erection faced with free-stone, on a plan so extraordinary, that it has puzzled persons, much better skilled in architecture than I pretend to be, to decide what class it belongs to. The mansion is a perfect square; on a line with the back front extends a string of offices, forming one wing under a colonnade, and thereby giving an air of deformity to the whole. The principal front recedes a little in the centre, for no reason but to countenance the erection of a modern balcony with a light iron railing, to contrast the gothic columns running up in the other

parts of the building. The windows are much too narrow and the grand saloon, which is of magnified dimensions, is completely spoiled by a rows small lights, like the windows of an attic story passing over the cornice and principal sash, besides all, the eye is offended by a line of battlements, above which rises a pointed and slated roof, giving a direct contradiction to the armed pretensions of the front; nor is this the worst error in judgment, for, amidst an assemblage of chimneys, roofs, cornices, and carved work, springs up a round Gothic tower, with long sash windows between the loop-holes, the only visible use of which strange excrescent is to sustain a flag-staff, whence the colours are occasionally displayed.[11]

In the Napoleonic Wars, as in the previous American War of Independence, the Island raised regiments of Fencibles (derived from the word 'defencible') for home defence. They also raised volunteer regiments, and although little

Castle Mona, now a hotel but once the residence of the Duke of Atholl

remains from these formations in terms of buildings, some of their gaudy uniforms may be found on display in the Mann at War gallery at the **Manx Museum**. During this era, however, it was the Royal Navy rather than the army which attracted Manxmen. Not all went willingly, and the activities of the press gang on the Island created great unrest at the time. However, as the wars went on and naval pay improved, many Manx seafarers came to see the Royal Navy as a good career choice. The most notable of these is Captain John Quilliam, who enlisted in the Royal Navy in 1792 as an able seaman. He rose rapidly through the ranks and was commissioned as a lieutenant. His abilities brought him to the attention of Lord Nelson, who requested that he serve with him aboard HMS *Victory*. He was present aboard her at the Battle of Trafalgar in 1805, and Manx legend has it that after the wheel of the *Victory* was shot away, Quilliam used his knowledge of ship

The monument on Douglas Head to the Manxmen who served at the Battle of Trafalgar in 1805

construction to create a jury rig to move her rudder and steer her. Research indicates that around sixty-six Manxmen served under Nelson at Trafalgar, and a monument on Douglas Head unveiled on the 200th anniversary of the battle ensures that they are not forgotten.

Quilliam's prize money enabled him to become a landed gentleman, and he was invited to become a member of the House of Keys. His Castletown home still survives, **Balcony House** on the square. An early account of it states:

> It has a fine ironwork balcony and a nice fanlight over the front door. Inside there were splendid mahogany doors, which have been removed. The drawing room on the first floor had elegant plaster elipses on the walls, which were difficult to see in Victorian days because of the trinkets.[12]

Other accounts recall the dressing rooms with their wig cupboards at the top of the house. On the first floor the front room ran the length of the building, and was designed originally as a ballroom. It had a reinforced floor, Italianate plasterwork and an Adams fireplace. Another story has it that the chimney was built such that the wind would whistle down it and remind Captain Quilliam of his time aboard ship!

The house is a stone's throw from the **Old House of Keys**, the former home of the Manx parliament, where Quilliam sat in his later years. Now it is operated as a visitor attraction by Manx National Heritage. This building was designed by Thomas Brine, the architect of many fine buildings in Castletown. Previously the Keys had met in what had been Bishop Wilson's Library, which was described as 'mean and decayed' and was clearly unsatisfactory. After a number of false starts, and plans rejected as too expensive, eventually the site of the library was purchased and Brine's revised design completed in 1821. However the Keys would occupy it only until 1874, before moving to Douglas.

Behind the Old House of Keys stands a fine and impressive building with a flight of five sandstone steps leading up to a door flanked by fluted pilasters. Originally there was also a sturdy pair of iron railings, since removed. This was formerly the **Royal Oak Inn**. It was built in the early or middle years of the eighteenth century and was said to have been the residence of Robert Kelly, who was High Bailiff of Castletown from 1808 to 1825. Though it is recorded as an inn in the middle years of the nineteenth century, by the latter part it had reverted to being a private house, the departure of the Keys to Douglas having no doubt removed the need for hotel accommodation in this part of the town.

As a member of the House of Keys, Quilliam sat alongside his friend Captain George Quayle. Quayle was a remarkable man – he held a captaincy in a Fencible regiment, paid for by his wealthy father, but was a merchant and banker in his own right, establishing the Island's first bank, and also an eccentric inventor and amateur scientist. His most famous existing creation is the *Peggy,* the world's oldest surviving yacht. As well as being a pleasure craft, she was fitted out with sliding keels, an experimental device also being studied by the Royal Navy at the time (*Peggy* is believed to have been the only civilian craft ever fitted with the technology). In his later years, through Quilliam's contacts at the Admiralty, Quayle was trying to interest the Royal Navy in a system of steam propulsion which he had developed. Like Quilliam's residence, Quayle's home – the imposing **Bridge House** – is now privately owned and not accessible to the public. However his remarkable boathouse, built to accommodate the *Peggy*, is now operated as the **Nautical Museum** by Manx National Heritage, and is open during the summer. The other impressive features of Castletown are the **Smelt monument**, constructed in 1836 to honour the memory of Lieutenant Governor Cornelius Smelt, and **St Mary's church**, built on the square between 1824 and 1826 to serve the garrison of the town. It was also designed by Thomas Brine, the architect responsible for the House of Keys in Parliament Square, as well as alterations to the castle, and probably the George Inn. He came from Glasgow and had settled on the Island with the Barrack Department some fifteen years before. In designing the church, he offered his services for nothing. The building is a fine example of Gothic revival, although it lost the upper stage of its tower in the early twentieth century. Today only the facade survives, the interior having been converted into offices in the 1980s. However we have a good description of what the church once looked like:

> The interior still contains the Governor's and family pews. These pews helped to raise money for the building of the Church. There is a receipt from E. M. Gawne of Kentraugh for M. H. Quayle who had purchased a pew from him

> in 1849 – 'Received from Mark H. Quayle this 16th March, 1849 a check on the prs. Holmes Douglas, for thirty six pounds sterling being the price of a double and single pew in St. Mary's Chapel Castletown and underneath the gallery, which I have this day sold to him.' On the walls of the Church are a fine selection of monuments ... [13]

It replaced an earlier church on the same site, which contained one of the first organs on the Isle of Man (only that at St George's in Douglas was older). This church was at the centre of Castletown society at the time, one newspaper of the day reporting on a concert held in 1811:

> On Tuesday the 31st ulto. at Castletown Chapel a grand Oratorio of Sacred Music was performed for the benefit of Mr. Gray, the Organist, upon which occasion nearly 'fifty guineas' were collected. It was numerously and most respectably attended. Personages of the first rank and fashion honoured the occasion with their presence, and were highly gratified. In short the whole performance could not fail to afford universal satisfaction.[14]

Overall, the genteel air of Georgian refinement still pervades Castletown square and the approaches to it, and the town has been luckier than others on the Island in that most of its finer buildings from this era survive, largely intact. It remained the seat of power under the new regime as it had under the Atholls, the mighty form of Castle Rushen brooding over the town and surrounding countryside. It would not be until the next century that a new wave of prosperity overtook the Island, taking the status of capital away to the new commercial centre – Douglas.

CHAPTER 4

The Victorians

With the ending of the Napoleonic wars, many retired half-pay officers found that their limited means went much further on the Isle of Man, where prices were considerably cheaper. Large numbers took up residence on the Island, and formed the core of the gentry in the early Victorian period in Douglas and Castletown. One such officer was Sir William Hillary. From his home at **Fort Anne** beside Douglas harbour he was witness to numerous shipwrecks on the treacherous Manx coast, and even assisted in some rescue attempts. This, and the fact that the families of would-be rescuers were often left destitute if they were to perish in the attempt, led him to campaign for the founding of a national organisation for saving life at sea. The Royal National Lifeboat Institution was his creation, but it was not his only legacy, for in Douglas he paid for the construction of the picturesque **Tower of Refuge** on Conister Rock, in Douglas Harbour. The rock had claimed a number of lives, and the tower was intended to provide shelter for shipwrecked mariners until help could arrive. In its early years it was stocked with provisions, though since its construction it has never been used for its intended purpose. Hillary was so taken with its crenelated style that he commissioned the same architect to build similar walls and turrets around his own property, an extravagance which eventually bankrupted him. Fort Anne occupies a commanding position on Douglas Head and although it was at one time a hotel, it is not currently open to the public. Nonetheless, good views of the walls and turrets can be had from the deck of a ferry entering or departing the harbour on a clear day. Hillary's impressive tomb, meanwhile, can be found in **St George's churchyard** in Douglas.

In 1832, the same year that Hillary constructed the Tower of Refuge, Douglas was hit by an outbreak of cholera which was making its way across Europe. The location of the pit used to bury the dead can still be seen in

The Tower of Refuge, in Douglas bay. It was constructed by Sir William Hillary to provide a shelter for shipwrecked mariners

St George's churchyard, between two simple wooden crosses. Katherine Forrest, writing some years later, describes the impact of the disease, and of the one woman who, without thought for herself, tended the dying:

> In Douglas was the greatest mortality; and at night in St George's churchyard the burial of the dead, as described by eyewitnesses, was a mournful and appalling sight never to be forgotten. There, by dim lanterns held in the hand, or suspended from the trees, the graves were dug, and in many cases the uncoffined bodies heaped in one after the other, and no stone ever to record more than one word – CHOLERA, close to the south-west entrance of St George's Church, a large memorial stone, railed round, is erected to commemorate the dreadful time. Engraven upon it is a lengthy record of the event, surrounded by a sculptured relieve, illustrating the horrors of pestilence.

> This was a period, indeed, to test the philanthropy and devotion of all those who had made profession of love to God and man, and truly many noble instances there were of self-denying efforts on behalf of the sufferers; but one name stands out prominently in the annals of the time, that is the name of the poor mangle-woman, Nelly Brennan.
>
> Where none but clergymen and doctors would dare to venture to alleviate anguish of body, and misery and despair of mind, Nelly would make her way. In seeking not her life, she found it; while others who sought to save, lost it. Nelly preserved her health, as if by miracle, all through the continuance of the plague.[15]

Nelly Brennan was to become known as 'the Florence Nightingale of the Isle of Man'. Like Hillary, she too is buried in St George's churchyard, where her headstone may still be seen.

During the Napoleonic Wars it had been impossible for the gentry to undertake the fashionable Grand Tour of Europe, upon which so many had embarked in the eighteenth century. Instead, these people began to take an interest in the wilder extremities of the British Isles, for example the Highlands of Scotland. A few of the more intrepid made it as far as the Isle of Man, and there are several accounts of tours through the Island which were published in this era.

With the coming of peace in 1815, however, what had begun as a trickle quickly became a torrent. Unlike modern tourists jetting off to the Spanish costas or Greek islands, the earliest holidaymakers were not in pursuit of a suntan as the yardstick of a successful vacation. Instead, these Victorian visitors were drawn to the Isle of Man because of the purity of its air, which contrasted greatly with the smoky conditions to be found in Britain's growing industrial cities, and for the health-giving properties of sea bathing. The technological advances of the Industrial Revolution also made access to the Island easier, with the establishment in 1830 of the Isle of Man Steam Packet Company (IoMSPCo), offering a regular scheduled steamer service to the Island from north-west England and southern Scotland. Other rival steamer services came and went, but the IoMSPCo was the most consistent and successful. Indeed, today it is the world's oldest shipping company still in operation.

Queen Victoria's visit to the Island in 1847 put the royal seal of approval on what was at that time still the exclusive preserve of the wealthy. Although Her Majesty remained on the Royal Yacht, Prince Albert was rowed ashore at Ballure near Ramsey, where he made his way up the glen. He was guided to Lhergy Frissel, where he climbed to the top of the hill. There he viewed the panorama of Ramsey and the northern plain. The hill was renamed Albert Mount in his honour, and a year later the foundation of the **Albert Tower** was laid to commemorate the visit. Made of granite and rising 45ft high, the tower stands as a landmark not only for the town of Ramsey, but for the Isle of Man as a whole. The paths to the tower are rather challenging, but do go right up to it. Access is through Lhergy Frissel Glen or other footpaths close by the Hairpin Corner. The tower itself is closed to the public, but visitors can take a good look at it from the outside, and of course can admire the view enjoyed by Prince Albert.

Where the aristocracy lead, the middle classes soon follow and not far behind them come the working classes. Before long tourism had mushroomed to become the staple industry of the Island. Some 90 per cent of its resident population were dependent on tourism by the time of the First World War. It is no exaggeration to say that the visiting industry was to the Isle of Man what coal was to the north east or cotton was to Lancashire. The numbers visiting the Island grew year on year, with the record figure of 660,000 being set in 1913; 1914 was on course to break that record, had the outbreak of war not intervened.

It is interesting to note that most of the architecture and infrastructure of the Isle of Man is the product of that tourist boom. Although the arc of Douglas Bay was dominated by large seafront hotels, the backbone of the accommodation sector was provided by smaller family-run guest houses. Many parts of Douglas are characterised not by the squat terraced housing of northern English industrial cities, but by taller, elegant three-storey terraces, which provided not only living quarters for the family, but perhaps four additional bedrooms which would be let to visitors in the summer months. Another product of the Victorian tourist boom was the world's first holiday camp. Liverpool-born Joseph Cunningham opened his fledgling camp for young male holidaymakers at Howstrake in 1894. So successful was it that in 1904 he acquired a larger plot on Victoria Road in Douglas. It could

Douglas at the height of the tourist boom, at the turn of the Twentieth Century. (Library of Congress)

accommodate 1,500 tents and a permanent dining pavilion. Despite the slurs and claims of immoral behaviour levelled against it by the jealous boarding-house keepers, Cunningham was a strict teetotaller who insisted on no alcohol in his camp. Yet despite its size and popularity, little remains of it now.

Much additional infrastructure grew up to serve the needs of the tourist industry. At one time Douglas boasted cinemas, theatres, the Derby Castle entertainment complex and the Palace ballroom (the largest covered dance floor in Europe), all providing entertainment for visitors. Most of the top names in variety appeared on the Isle of Man, and many of the shows which toured the seaside holiday resorts began their run here. Sadly, now only the **Gaiety Theatre** and the **Villa Marina** survive, but the lavishly restored Gaiety is one of the best surviving examples of a Victorian music hall anywhere in the British Isles. Regular productions, both amateur and professional, are still staged at the Gaiety and frequent 'behind the scenes' tours (on Saturdays during the summer) offer a chance to explore the understage trap doors and other parts of the building not usually accessible.

The Villa Marina began life as a private house, constructed by Robert Steuart (son of the architect). Later in the nineteenth century it served as a select boarding school, before once again becoming a private house, this time the home of Henry Bloom Noble. Noble was one of the Island's greatest benefactors, and having made a great deal of money in business, endowed the Island's hospital as well as providing a library and playing fields. In his will he left Douglas Corporation the option to purchase the property for development as a tourist attraction, and in 1913 the new building was officially opened by Lord Raglan. In the *Manx Quarterly* it was stated that the new building was to cater,

> ... for a class of holiday-maker whom we in Douglas have hitherto been neglectful of. Large numbers of our visitors care little or nothing for dancing and variety turns, nor do exhibitions of cinematography appeal to them with any great amount of force. Nevertheless they appreciate entertainment more staid and perchance more elevating of character, and this is just the sort of entertainment which it is intended to provide in connection with the beautiful gardens and hall which are owned by the Corporation of Douglas.[16]

However the German-sounding name of Kursaal was quickly dropped following the outbreak of war, and the old title was readopted. Another superbly restored Victorian gem is the **Camera Obscura** on Douglas Head. Originally built in the 1890s, it uses only lenses and natural light to project images of the surrounding vista. It was said that when it was first constructed, a large part of the attraction for visitors was the ability to spy on courting couples on Douglas Head; now it is one of only around four of these Victorian kaleidoscopes which survive in the British Isles.

Many of the other tourist attractions on Douglas Head, such as the Gypsy Encampment or the rollercoaster, did not reopen after the Second World War. Similarly, the Marine Drive tramway that once took summer visitors from Douglas Head to Port Soderick and back, also closed due to the war and was dismantled afterwards. Today only the impressive brick and

The Camera Obscura on Douglas Head, seen during its Victorian heyday

stone arch which once marked the start of the line survives. Another rail network built to serve tourists fortunately did make it to the present day, and that is the **Douglas Bay Horse Tramway.** It was established in 1876 by an enterprising Douglas businessman in order to collect visitors from their steamer in Douglas harbour, and deliver them to their hotel further up the Promenade. The business was soon acquired by Douglas Corporation, and the iconic 'toastrack' trams still run along Douglas Promenade in the summer to this day, making it the oldest horse-drawn tramway system in the world still in operation. The horse tramway stables are located at the northern end of the Promenade and are sometimes open for tours.

As the visiting industry grew, so the horse tramway came to connect with the route of the Douglas cable-car company, enabling visitors and their luggage to reach boarding houses further from the sea front, and to the electric and steam railways, allowing tourists to reach accommodation in Port Erin, Peel or Ramsey. It was the world's first integrated public transport system, and both the steam railway line to Port Erin, and the **Manx Electric Railway** (MER) are preserved and in operation each summer. The ornate red brick facade of **Douglas station** is worth seeing even if your time does not permit a journey south on the steam railway to explore Castletown, Ballasalla or the **Railway Museum** at Port Erin. Intriguingly, from Ronaldsway Halt it is possible to reach the airport, making it the only international airport in the world which is served by a regular scheduled steam train service. In its Victorian heyday the network was much more extensive, with a Peel line from Douglas, which connected with the Manx Northern Railway at St Johns. From here, passengers could reach Ramsey via Sulby.

The Manx Electric Railway was established in 1893, and two of the original cars are still in operation, making them the oldest such vehicles still in use on their original line in the world. A museum dedicated to the history of the MER can be found at the Derby Castle depot, at the end of Queens Promenade. Admission is free, and the museum is open on Sundays when the railway is in operation. Trains depart the Douglas terminus for Ramsey,

A 1930s poster advertising the Manx Electric Railway

with various stops along the way including the quaint **Laxey station**. From here it is possible to catch the service for Snaefell summit. On a clear day, the views as the carriage ascends the mountain can be breathtaking, but even on a not so fine day, riding in an original Victorian carriage with its gleaming woodwork and brass fittings is a delight for nostalgia lovers. It is a popular Manx saying that from the summit of Snaefell one can see six kingdoms – the kingdom of Heaven, the kingdom of the sea, the kingdom of Mann, and of course England, Scotland and Ireland. The growth in the transport network in the Victorian era encouraged entrepreneurs to open other tourist attractions. One such was Groudle Glen at Onchan, where a scenic walk through a river valley was enhanced by the addition of tea rooms, and a small zoo containing polar bears and sealions. To link these attractions to the MER line, a narrow-gauge railway was built through the glen in 1896. Hugely popular with visitors in the early twentieth century, the zoo did not reopen after the Second World War and the line soon fell into abeyance. In recent years, however, a dedicated team of volunteers have restored both the line and the miniature engines, and a visit to the **Groudle Glen Railway** is now a must for any steam buff, particularly narrow-gauge fans. Transport enthusiasts should also be sure to visit the **Manx Heritage Transport Museum** at Jurby where, as well as numerous historic buses, an example of a cable tram can be found.

Though tourism was the mainstay of the economy in this era, the geology of the Isle of Man also meant that it had rich seams of lead and zinc ore. Both metals were key components of the Industrial Revolution and the expansion of the Victorian age. There were two main mining sites on the Island, at Foxdale and at Laxey. Mining engineers encountered problems at the latter in particular, because of the high water-table and the fact that the richest seam was under the Laxey River. Because of another peculiarity of Manx geology, the fact that there was no naturally occurring coal on the Island, steam power was not widely used. Instead, Manx engineers used bigger and bigger waterwheels to try to pump the unwanted water from the Laxey mine. The ultimate result of this was the colossal **Great Laxey Wheel** (or 'Lady Isabella' – named after the wife of the Lieutenant Governor of the day) which was completed in 1854. With the construction of this enormous wheel – still the Isle of Man's greatest piece of industrial archaeology – two

THE VICTORIANS 49

The Groudle Glen sealions, seen on a postcard from the late Nineteenth Century

industries came together, for Laxey was on the tourist route to Ramsey, and very soon a visit to the great wheel became an essential part of the itinerary. So numerous were the visitors that by the 1870s a subsidiary catering industry had developed; 'Ham and Egg terrace' in Laxey village acquired its nickname from the many cafés which sprang up there.

The other features dominating the village were the 'deads'. The huge spoil heaps contained waste products from mining, such as quartz and other semi precious stones which were extracted alongside the valuable ore. Tourists began taking away pieces of quartz as souvenirs, and so the more enterprising miners used this waste material to fashion elaborate 'spar boxes', which were then sold to the wealthier visitors. Another by-product of the mine was silver, the ore of which frequently occurs alongside lead ore, but at Laxey it was never found in sufficient quantities to make it a staple part of the economy. However, the truth seldom gets in the way of a good story, and the cafés soon began selling a range of 'Laxey Silver' products – spoons, forks, sugar tongs and other items, all silver plated ... and all made in Birmingham.

Today a visit to the Laxey Wheel is still an essential part of the visitor experience when coming to the Isle of Man for the first time. The wheel can be seen from quite a distance while still in the village itself and, nestled in a picturesque glen, it exemplifies the Victorian attitude that man's God-given mission was to conquer nature, in much the same way that the Ribblehead Viaduct strides magnificently across the beautiful North Yorkshire countryside.

The wheel itself is maintained by Manx National Heritage and is open from Easter to around October (check the MNH website for the latest information and details of admission prices). Today it is sometimes difficult for visitors to appreciate the hustle and bustle of this now sleepy village in its mining heyday, though the story of the miners is well-told by interpretation panels around the site. The more hardy visitor (or at least those with sturdy footwear) can make a short trek (about half a mile) up the valley both to get a better view of the T-rocker which would have operated the pumps, and also the site of the Man Engine, an astonishing piece of Victorian engineering which allowed miners to descend the 2,000ft or so to the working levels by stepping on and off a constantly moving ladder. In addition, a short stretch of adit (a mine tunnel cut straight into the Manx rock face) is usually open to visitors. For getting a feel for the cramped and wet working conditions –

The Great Laxey Wheel, believed to be the world's largest working waterwheel. (Library of Congress)

and the ever-present danger from rock falls – this has to be experienced. Laxey resident Egbert Rydings made a descent into the mine in the 1880s, and described it in a contemporary guidebook. Although he entered via the Main Adit, not the Old Adit which visitors can explore today, the account is still highly atmospheric:

> The entrance is very difficult, being a narrow path on which the wagons run and which is not very dry in any season, but over this some three or four hundred people have to travel over eighty yards to and from work. Walking over the rails or in the pump water we eventually reached the end of the level. Then we came to where the descent commences on the ladders. I had put on a pair of old trousers and a greatcoat to cover my white shirt, but then the command was given, 'off with thy coat and waist coat' and from the nature of the entrance to the deep mine, I saw that this was absolutely necessary, for the hole was not more than two feet square. Having lit our candles and stuck them in front of our stiff felt hats we prepared to descend. My guide led the way with repeated injunctions to 'hold fast with your hands' and 'step onto the ladder.' No sooner do our heads pass through the hole than out go the lights and we are left in darkness. Attempts to relight the candles failed until at last the guide had to take a candle in his hand and hold it against his breast to keep the wind from blowing it out. I must confess I felt considerably shaky going down the ladders as straight as the sides of a well and in darkness. I found, too, that some of the spokes were feeling quite loose and many of the iron binding spokes were worn quite thin as to feel like dull knives. And to make matters worse, the spokes were made slippery from the accumulation of clay and wet. We have now got to the bottom of the first set of ladders and, as the draught of air rushing down the shaft is not so strong, the candles can be lit again. I find it much easier now as I can see the ladder and the hands can grasp it more certainly. But let us remark that the light of a candle penetrates such a short distance into the surrounding darkness that you cannot see around you more than four or five yards; and well it is so in climbing these fearful ladders.[17]

On the floor of the Old Adit can be seen original rails from the mines tramway. In the early nineteenth century, pit ponies had been used to haul the ore out of the mine for processing, but later the company purchased two miniature steam locomotives for this, known as the Ant and the Bee because of their small but industrious nature. The original engines were scrapped long ago, but in summer time the **Laxey Mines Railway** operates two faithful replica engines along a restored section of track. In addition, a group of local enthusiasts have re-established a small water wheel, the 'Lady Evelyn', in the centre of the village, on what was once the mine washing floor, where the ore was crushed and sorted. At the Manx Museum in Douglas there is also a small display of mining artefacts, including an original ore truck recovered from deep within the mine.

The other main Manx industry in this era was fishing, and it was said that in the 1880s one third of the Manx population was reliant on it, or its associated trades such as net making. Nowhere was this more true that in Peel, where tradition had it that at the height of the industry it was possible to walk from one side of the harbour to the other simply by passing from one fishing boat to the next, so tightly were they packed. Many of the fish caught were herring, which were subsequently smoked as kippers. Kippers were once the Isle of Man's most famous export, and are still served with marmalade for breakfast in the Island's hotels. Only one traditional kipper smoking house survives on the Island, **Moore's Kipper Yard** in Peel, and guided tours are sometimes available. Check the company website for details of when and how to book. The story of kipper production, and of Peel's fishing industry as a whole are explored in the **Leece Museum**, and also at **House of Manannan** on Peel's harbourside, where other aspects of the Island's maritime culture such as the impact of the Isle of Man Steam Packet Company on local life are covered.

To get a real sense of what domestic life was like in Victorian times on the Isle of Man, visit the **Grove** at Ramsey. This small mansion was originally purchased by Duncan Gibb, a wealthy Liverpool shipping magnate, as a holiday home for his wife and children in the 1840s. He extended the house, added an imposing frontage to impress his visitors, and developed it as a working farm. Gradually the family became full-time residents, and the last members to live here were Janet and Alice Gibb, Duncan's granddaughters. The two sisters were unmarried, and had no desire for the house to be divided up into flats or demolished for redevelopment after their deaths, so they approached the trustees of the Manx Museum to see if an arrangement could

The Grove Museum at Ramsey. Once the home of the Gibb family, the house retains many of its original contents

be reached. In due course, the museum acquired the house and its contents, of which there were many. After two years of sorting and cataloguing the objects within, the property reopened as the Grove Museum.

What makes the Grove particularly interesting is the fact that unlike many other Victorian museums in the UK, where an empty shell has been filled with representative objects, almost every item which is on display at this museum was used by the Gibb family. Indeed, photographs exist of some of the rooms as they appeared in the nineteenth century, so the manner in which they are set out is known to be accurate. The 'upstairs, downstairs' world of the Victorian gentry is explored in the grand dining and drawing rooms, kitchen, scullery and spartan servants' quarters. Friendly and helpful staff are on hand to advise visitors about the displays, and tell them more about the lives of the Gibbs.

At the other end of the social spectrum, **Cregneash Folk Museum** offers insights into the lives of ordinary Manx crofting families in the nineteenth century. Britain's first open-air museum, it began life in the 1930s when the Manx Museum acquired the home of Harry Kelly, a local crofter who was believed to be the last 'native' Manx speaker. As a stronghold of the Manx language, the village was already attracting tourists, scholars, and enthusiasts alike when Carl Marstrander, Professor of Celtic at the University of Oslo, made the first sound recordings of Manx speech with Harry Kelly. His home has come to personify the simple Manx cottage, with its two front windows and centrally placed doorway opening straight into the main living space, with its large open kitchen hearth ('chiollagh'). To one side a door opens into the only other room, which served as a bed space, with a half-loft above which could be used as extra sleeping accommodation or for storage. Even a simple cottage such as this has a history of change and adaptation built into it, however, as an examination of the rear wall shows that it once had a back door as well. In days gone by, when wheat was threshed on the floor of the cottage, opening both doors would have allowed the chaff to blow out.

The underside of the thatched roof is open to see, with the characteristic underlay of turf 'scraa' preserved by years of peat smoke. Above this, layers of wheat straw provide an effective weatherproof seal, even against the strong winds that blow through the village. Viewed from outside, the web of ropes holding the thatch in place clearly shows how this local technique of thatching has been made to work, despite the difficult climate.

This simple whitewashed thatched cottage was regarded as iconic by the museum authorities as it represented the way of life of the ordinary Manx people in the Victorian era. These people subsisted on a smallholding which they farmed themselves, perhaps with one or two animals, selling any surplus butter or cheese at market, or supplementing their income by fishing when the season was right (the traditional diet of the Manx was said to be 'spuds and herring'). Over time, other dwellings in the village have been acquired and the museum has grown. Church Farm demonstrates a more sophisticated and prosperous method of agriculture, while Cummal Beg was originally a single storey cottage, with an upper floor added in the twentieth century.

The low intensity, traditional methods of farming at Cregneash are intended not just to preserve these skills for their own sake, but also to return the countryside in this part of the Island to the appearance that it would have had over 100 years ago, when it was managed very differently.

The interior of Harry Kelly's cottage, Cregneash. When it was acquired by the Manx Museum it was probably unique in that rather than being the seat of a prince or a lord, it was the typical home of an ordinary working man

By and large, however, life on the land was harsh, and from the 1840s onwards successive waves of emigration saw Manx people leave the countryside in large numbers. By the 1930s, some of the cottages at Cregneash were already being used only as summertime holiday lets. Many of those leaving the land headed for the United States, with Ohio in particular being a favourite destination. (Today, it is said that there are more people of Manx descent in the Cleveland area than there are on the Isle of Man.) While driving around the Island, you may well see roofless stone-built cottages dotted across the countryside. Known as Tholtans, these are silent monuments to the many thousands who left their homeland in this era. Indeed, so important are they considered to the Manx national memory and consciousness, that it is forbidden to renovate them.

The most famous resident of the Isle of Man in the Victorian era was undoubtedly the author Hall Caine. Although he has been almost entirely forgotten now, Hall Caine was one of the biggest literary names of his age. Indeed, his popularity in his lifetime is hard to overstate. He wrote fifteen novels, and sold 10 million books, including the first novel to sell over a million copies. He drew inspiration from Manx history and culture, and many of his works became Broadway or West End productions, while others were filmed. The 1929 adaptation of *The Manxman* for example was an early work by Alfred Hitchcock. Among his contacts and correspondents were Bram Stoker and Dante Gabriel Rosetti. Hall Caine lived at **Greeba Castle** on the road to Peel, which although privately owned can be glimpsed through the trees from the road. He died in 1931, and is buried at Maughold churchyard. Although commercially he was very successful, critically his work has not withstood the test of time, as for example has that of Charles Dickens.

As the nineteenth century drew to a close a new artistic movement was gathering strength. Called Art Noveau, in many respects it drew its inspiration from what its proponents saw as a simpler way of life in the past. In the Isle of Man, two of the greatest exponents of this new wave of design were the architect Mackay Hugh Baillie-Scott, and the artist Archibald Knox. Both would become internationally recognised for their work individually, but on the Isle of Man they sometimes worked collaboratively. It was said that Baillie-Scott had come to the Island for his honeymoon, but was so seasick on the way over that he could not face going back. He designed a number of buildings which are still extant on the Island, including **Onchan Parish Hall**, and **Castletown Police Station**. He also designed a number of private houses, including **Thornbank** in Douglas, which is now owned by Manx National Heritage (access by appointment only). Baillie-Scott believed that in medieval times the hall had been the central feature of the home, and that it had become unjustly relegated to a simple passageway between other rooms. His private houses placed the hall once more at the centre of the home. His ornate woodwork and other features also reflected what he saw as an earlier golden age of architecture.

Archibald Knox, meanwhile, was the Manx-born son of a Douglas engineer. He drew inspiration from the Celtic heritage of the Isle of Man (particularly its carved stones) and would often spend hours wandering alone in the countryside, seeking to reconnect with the Celtic past. His work at the end of the nineteenth and beginning of the twentieth century fitted closely into a wider revival of interest in all things Celtic, which was driven by figures such as Charles Rennie Mackintosh and the Glasgow School of Art circle. Although Knox was an accomplished watercolourist, it seems that he thought little of his landscape artworks and often gave them away. However it was as a designer, particularly for the London firm of Liberty, that he really shone. He devised a scheme of pewterware, which he called Tudric, and silverware which he called Cymric. The elegant, flowing designs incorporated leaves and flowers, often embellished with enamel or semi-precious stones. Today these objects are highly sought after and command high prices at auction. After spells living near London, Knox eventually returned to the Isle of Man where he also designed gravestones, war memorials and letterheads. His home, on Athol Street in Douglas, was lost in a road-widening scheme, but today the **Archibald Knox garden** occupies part of the site. A blue plaque on the wall here commemorates the fact that in 1933 Knox died in the house which once stood on this spot.

Less well known than Knox, but arguably a rival claimant for the title of the greatest Manx artist, is John Miller Nicholson. Numbers of his works are to be found in the Manx Museum, but probably his most impressive commission (and one which reflects his origins as a house painter) is **St Thomas's church** on Finch Road in Douglas. The building was designed in the Victorian early Gothic style, by architect Ewan Christian. The foundation stone was laid in 1846 and the church was opened in August 1849. However, between 1896 and 1910 the walls of the chancel and nave were elaborately painted by Nicholson. Using the then vicar Canon Savage's ideas, the church was transformed by the unique and magnificent murals which he created. Covering some 520 square metres of wall space, these decorative paintings remain St Thomas' most outstanding artistic feature and are well worth a visit. Other notable features of the church include the war memorial designed by Archibald Knox, several beautiful stained glass windows, the three manual organs and the bell and clock tower.

Politically, in the late Victorian and Edwardian eras, the Isle of Man was more advanced than the United Kingdom in several ways. Having an independent parliament effectively gave the Manx people Home Rule (though within the constraints imposed by a Lieutenant Governor appointed from Westminster). This was at a time when Irish nationalist politicians were pressing for a similar arrangement with the British government, and the Isle of Man was held up as an example of a way by which Irish aspirations might be satisfied, while that country remained within the fold of the British Empire. Many tracts and documents of this era referred to the Isle of Man as 'The Land of Home Rule'. The Manx were also ahead of the UK in that women of property on the Island had been entitled to vote in elections since 1881. Indeed, the noted suffragist campaigner Emmeline Pankhurst came from a Manx family. Her mother was born Sophia Jane Craine in Lonan, and her family ran boarding houses in Douglas. Although Emmeline was born in Manchester, she was a regular visitor to her mother's family on the Isle of Man. The contrast in status between women in England and the Isle of Man cannot have escaped her notice, and it is widely believed that this contributed to her political activism. Sophia moved back to the Isle of Man with Emmeline's brother, and until her death in 1910 lived at a house on **Strathallen Crescent** in Douglas. A blue plaque outside the house now commemorates its connection with Emmeline Pankhurst.

As the nineteenth century came to an end, the Isle of Man's place as Britain's premier holiday destination looked assured. A construction boom was in full swing, as builders struggled to keep up with the demand for new boarding houses, while a fleet of elegant modern steamships glided through the water between Douglas and surrounding coasts. With the dawn of the twentieth century, a new attraction would be added in the form of motor racing, but the dark clouds of war would soon gather over the holiday isle.

CHAPTER 5

The TT Races

The Isle of Man can with some justification claim to be the birthplace of two-, three- and four-wheeled motor racing. This started as early as 1904, with the Gordon Bennett eliminating trials for cars; while the Westminster parliament refused to allow roads to be closed for racing, Tynwald offered no such objections – indeed the potential of the races to attract tourists was noted from the outset. Roads were subsequently closed for the first Royal Automobile Club motorcar Tourist Trophy (TT) races, and from 1907 onward the Island also played host to the motorcycle TT, organised by the Auto Cycle Union (ACU). It is an aspect of the Island's history which has international significance, and as such merits its own chapter within this guidebook.

Following an approach by Julian Orde to the Lieutenant Governor, Lord Raglan, the RAC Tourist Trophy for motorcars was first held on the Isle of Man in 1905, and was staged here sporadically afterwards until 1922. Notable participants included the Honourable Charles Rolls (co-founder of Rolls Royce) who won in 1906, and Kenelm Lee Guinness (of the famous brewing family) who won in 1914. Other marques which competed here include Sunbeam, Bentley and Humber. The motorcycle race grew out of the motorcar event, and the programme for the 1907 ACU TT was actually just an insert in the programme for the latter.

With suspensions only for wartime and the outbreak of foot and mouth disease, the Isle of Man TT has taken place annually for over 111 years. In the 1920s it was joined by the Amateur Road Race, now known as the Manx Grand Prix, which takes place on the same course in August. There can be few other places in the world where a sporting event has developed such a close, and indeed symbiotic, relationship with the landscape in which it exists. The topography of the Isle of Man created the TT and gave it its character, while at the same time the races have impacted upon the landscape of the Island, influencing place names and other geographical features.

It had been intended that the proposed course for the earliest TT races should head south from Douglas towards Castletown, before turning west to Peel. However, the Isle of Man Railway refused to halt services at the Quarterbridge level crossing during racing, and so the course instead heads west out of Douglas, rather than south. The citizens of Peel objected to motorcycles hurtling through their narrow streets, so in 1911 the mountain section was adopted for the first time. The TT Mountain Course is now the oldest motorcycle racing circuit in the world which is still in use.

Many of the locations around the course have become etched into motorcycle lore, with several closely associated with a particular legendary rider. It is the character of this long and winding 37.75 mile course which sets it apart from the level and smooth short circuits of the world, and which endears it to many fans still today. There is no doubt that some people consider it dangerous – it is certainly unforgiving if a rider makes a mistake – and it has often aroused controversy as a result. Yet the fact that this type of race can only exist here (it is hard to imagine anything similar ever being set up in the UK) and that it does so sometimes in the face of UK

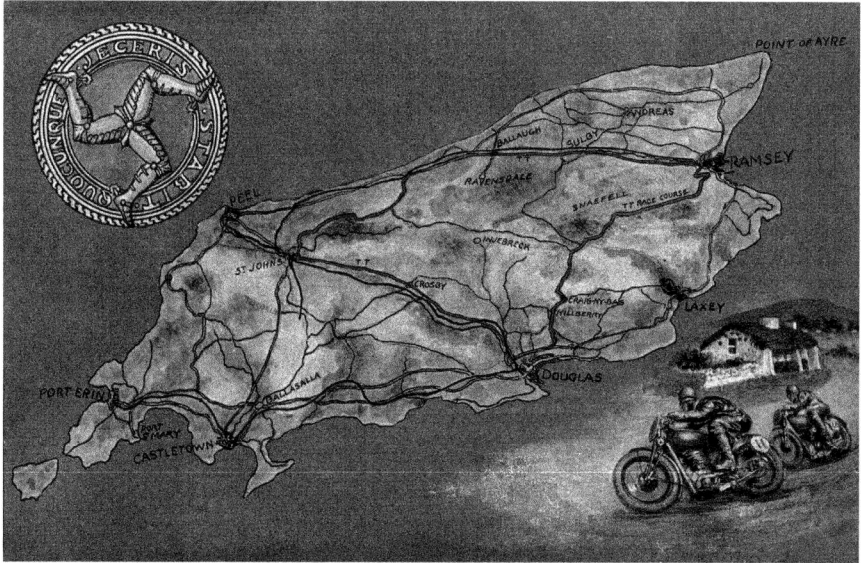

The TT course illustrated on a 1930s postcard

media criticism, is oddly characteristic of the fiercely independent nature of the Manx people. There is no doubt that in its long and illustrious history, the Manx have taken it strongly to heart, with over 70 per cent of the native population expressing support for it. It is now considered an essential part of what makes the Island unique. So without further ado, let us take a tour of the circuit, along the way meeting some of the people who have made the TT races what they are.

The races begin at the grandstand, on Glencrutchery Road. The present building dates from 1986, and replaced a wooden structure which had stood since the 1920s. The decision to replace the original grandstand came in the wake of serious fires at similar wooden structures in the UK around this time. The earlier building can be seen in the George Formby film *No Limit* (1936), and among the national flags fluttering above it in one particular scene, the swastika of Nazi Germany is clearly visible. Hitler and the Nazis sought TT glory for its propaganda value, of which more later.

If you are visiting out of season the grandstand will seem oddly quiet, almost forlorn. You can walk unhindered down the pit lane, and perhaps your imagination will allow you to conjure up a little of the frenzied atmosphere which exists here in 'gasoline alley' on race day. Races can be won or lost in the pits, and teams go to great efforts to ensure that tyre changes and refuelling are as slick as possible. In non-race periods you can also climb the steps of the winner's podium, and imagine yourself in the footsteps of your hero (believe it or not, the TT podium has even been used as a location for wedding photos!). Across the road is the scoreboard, which retains much the same form as when it was first set up here in the 1920s. The scoreboard is operated by scouts, who carry handwritten notes of lap times to signwriters who update the board manually. In today's digital age, all competing machines have transponders, which allow observers to track their progress on the internet in real time. When the information has been relayed to a signwriter, who then makes a number board to be put up on the scoreboard by a boy scout, it is largely historic, but there remains a groundswell of affection for this traditional and unique part of the race.

Now, head south from the grandstand, down towards Bray Hill. As you pass through St Ninian's crossroads, take a look to your right. This was once known as Parkfield Corner, when the minor Clypse Course was in use for a brief time in the 1950s and 1960s. It was on this course that the mighty Honda Motor Company first ventured into motorcycle racing, when the firm sent a team to compete in the 1959 TT. Soichiro Honda, founder of the company, had long admired the TT as the toughest test of a racing motorcycle anywhere in the world, and believed that if his machines could win here they could win anywhere. Although the first Honda riders were inexperienced, and their machines unproven, they still carried off the team prize that year. It was a remarkable achievement and marked the beginning of Honda's long association with the TT, as well as its global racing success. At the next set of traffic lights the road dips sharply, before starting to rise again. This is known as Ago's Leap. The slight gradient is named after Giacomo Agostini, who rode for the Italian firm of MV Agusta in the 1960s, and who would often have his front wheel in the air at this point. Agostini would go on to become world champion fifteen times. In a few hundred yards the road levels a little. You are now passing the original start line, in use before the First World War. Apart from a large house set back from the road on the right, few of the buildings here now were then present. In those days mechanics waited in the original 'pits', hollows on the right hand side of the road – a term which the Isle of Man has given to the world.

At the bottom of Bray Hill we come to Quarterbridge, a daunting right-hander for riders with a full tank of fuel attempting to slow for the turn. A popular viewing spot, in part due to the presence of the Quarterbridge Hotel, it is said that if you get it wrong here the crowd know before you do, as indicated by the fact that they start to move back from the barriers. Many inexperienced riders come unstuck here, and double world champion Barry Sheene famously slid off at Quarterbridge in his only TT appearance in 1971. Next we pass the Jubilee Oak, planted in honour of Queen Victoria, and sweep through Braddan Bridge, with the Joey Dunlop Foundation house for disabled riders on the right and the viewing area at Braddan church on the left. The next landmark is Union Mills, so named because it was once the location of both a corn and a textile mill. Up until the 1980s the entrance to Union Mills was much narrower, and presented more of a challenge to riders. However it was while exiting the village that the great Bob McIntyre almost came unstuck, during his famous 1957 Senior performance which broke the 100mph lap barrier; he was struck hard on the forehead by a stone, thrown up by the rear wheel of another motorcycle on the fifth lap. The injury is clearly apparent in photographs of McIntyre taken immediately afterwards. In writing about the race, he recalled that:

> [as] I accelerated away, a stone hit me, thrown up by the wheels of another rider I was about to lap. It was probably no bigger than a pea, but at 100mph it felt like a brick. It caught me between my goggles and my crash helmet and cut my left temple. I felt dazed and sick, it brought tears to my eyes and I felt blood running. But fortunately, the rush of cold air coagulated the blood above my goggles.[18]

After passing through Union Mills we reach Ballagarey, a bend located between the third and fourth milestones, and known to the riders of the current era as 'Ballascary'. It was the setting for a dramatic incident in 2010, when the machine ridden by Guy Martin crashed at high speed, with a full tank of fuel after a pit stop just minutes earlier, and exploded into a fireball. Martin escaped serious injury, and after being airlifted by helicopter, recovered in hospital from bruising to both lungs and minor fractures to his upper spine. Guy has since gone on to become one of Britain's most popular TV presenters, and one of the best-known motorcycle racers in the world.

After Glen Vine and Crosby (the pub of which name is a popular viewing spot), we pass the Highlander Inn. After swooping past Greeba Castle we quickly reach Ballacraine, another popular spectator location. Here the course sweeps sharply to the right. The large building on the far side of the junction was once the Ballacraine Hotel, and in *No Limit* a rider famously crashes through the front door and out of the back door, before rejoining the race. Indeed, many of the extras who appeared in the film were actual competitors, including the rider who executed that stunt. Here, we are on part of the St John's course, used for the first ever TT in 1907. This race was run over ten laps of the course, totalling some 158 miles. Passing Ballig Bridge and Doran's Bend (named after Bill Doran, who crashed here in both the 1950 and 1952 TT races) we sweep through Laurel Bank and Glen Helen. The sheer cliffs bordering the road here make this a section which has to be treated with utmost respect. Soon we pass Sarah's Cottage, named after a woman who once provided refreshments to the early TT riders.

Next comes Creg Willey's Hill, back in the Edwardian era undoubtedly the biggest challenge on the course, where in those days the road was narrow and winding. Most of the machines in the first ever TT were also equipped with pedals, and the usual approach to this apparently unassuming gradient (which nevertheless in this era represented a major difficulty) was to open the throttle wide at Glen Helen and build up as much speed as possible, then pedal the last few yards. The Devil's Elbow was also a treacherous part of the course if approached too fast, and many a rider came unstuck here. However, more than a century of infrastructure investment means that the quality of the road surface is now markedly different. The highway here in 1907 was not metalled, and the surface was loose and gritty. In dry weather, passing traffic was apt to stir up clouds of dust, so the TT organisers decided that the best course of action was to spray this stretch of road with an acid solution from a water cart. This had unexpected effects, in as much as not only did the acid fail to settle the swirling clouds of dust, it also burned holes in the riders' clothing. Triumph competitor Jack Marshall, who rode in the first ever TT race, remembered that the fine powdery surface presented another hazard:

> Overtaking was extremely difficult, not to say dangerous. One charged blindly into a cloud of dust and hoped that there would be a clear road ahead on the other side of it, and that the cause of the dust would not wobble or swerve as one went past.[19]

The long straight at Cronk Y Voddy is also a good viewing spot, and it was here that the exhaust of Carl Fogarty (arguably Britain's greatest living motorcycle racer, though now perhaps better remembered for winning *I'm a Celebrity – Get Me Out of Here!*) spectacularly disintegrated during his epic 1992 Senior TT battle against Steve Hislop. This encounter has been voted by fans as the greatest ever TT race; pieces of the exhaust wadding were seen all over the road, and Fogarty remembered:

> … the lead changed after every lap and I was riding so hard that the bike was falling apart around me. None of the clocks were working, the front fork seal had gone, the rear brake arm was bent up, the rear shock was broken – the bike was an absolute mess. I was nine seconds behind at the start of the final lap,

which was a lot to make up. To make matters worse, the exhaust blew coming over the mountain as I made that final push. After I had finished, I could hear the commentary over the tannoy, '... and here comes Hislop, he wins by four seconds ...'[20]

At the end of the Cronk Y Voddy straight we come to Molyneux's bend. Named in 2013, it honours Manxman Dave Molyneux, the most successful sidecar competitor in the history of the TT, whose career stretches over an incredible thirty years. Molyneux has been noted as one of the most successful constructors at the TT, building race-winning outfits for himself and other competitors. He also has the rare distinction of having won a TT race on each of the four major Japanese engines.

Drinkwater's and Handley's are both named after riders of earlier decades who came off here, while next we come to McGuinness's, again named in 2013 in honour of one of the greatest riders of modern times, John McGuinness. The so-called 'Morecambe Missile' was a Honda factory rider for a number of years, and dominated the event in the early twenty-first century. He was the first man to break the 130mph barrier, at the 2007 TT.

We now head towards Kirk Michael village, home of the Mitre Hotel, a famous watering hole giving views onto the course, which hurtles through the centre of the village and onwards to Ballaugh. In this latter village is located a famous humpbacked bridge. The dramatic leaps performed by riders and machines exiting the crest here have made for some incredible photos over the years. Near Ballaugh Bridge we find both the Raven pub, a popular venue for race fans which is adorned with racing memorabilia, and also a small bronze memorial for Karl Gall, a German rider killed in practice during the 1939 TT. In fact Gall was no ordinary competitor, but was a member of a paramilitary German motorcycle corps and a part of a squad which included 1939 Senior winner Georg Meier. They had been sent with the express ambition of achieving motorcycle racing glory for the Third Reich; their success that year constituted a propaganda victory to rank alongside the 1936 Berlin Olympics, and the world heavyweight boxing championship secured by Max Schmelling. The memorial is set into the gatepost of a house, the last in a white painted terrace across the road from the Raven.

After Quarry Bends we approach the Sulby Straight. In the 1930s Irish ace Stanley Woods (the first man to reach ten wins, and certain to have achieved more if the Second World War had not intervened) almost came a cropper near here:

> A spot of excitement on this last lap at Close Wood, near Sulby. Deschamps had parted company with his Norton on the grease under the trees. Before the road could be cleared I came along – at about 110mph. The road here takes a series of bends – right, left, right, left. I do not shut off until I am round the first right, then I brake slightly and engage third gear. Thereafter, I accelerate through the remainder of the bends, emerging on the approach to Sulby Straight at almost peak revs in third. Quite a nice place to find the road blocked! And that is just what I might have done if it had not been for the quick action of a lady spectator. She was standing on the apex of the first left bend, inside the hedge, and as I approached she waved a red hat violently in front of me. It looked a bit too agitated to be merely enthusiasm, so I eased up considerably and picked a course past the fallen rider with ease.[21]

On the Sulby Straight itself we find the Sulby Glen Hotel, nicknamed 'the German Embassy' because two German motorcycle clubs regularly camp in the field opposite during the TT races. Another favourite with fans, the hotel is run by Rosie Sayle whose son Dan is a TT racer. The next hostelry which we pass is the Ginger Hall, perhaps equally famous. The name derives from the fact that it once served homemade ginger beer. From here, we pass Milntown before heading into Ramsey.

Parliament Square in the town centre is another popular viewing spot, where again riders slow down, making it a good location for photography. This was the scene of a famous tussle between Mike Hailwood and his old adversary Phil Read, during the former's return to the TT. Hailwood had competed on the Island in the 1960s, and in 1967 set a lap record which stood for eight years. After an eleven-year break in which he raced cars, he sensationally returned to the TT in 1978. In the Formula 1 race that year, Hailwood had started as number 12, while Read (riding a factory Honda) was tipped to win. As he approached Ramsey, Read took a quick look over his shoulder to find that Hailwood had caught him, and the two were neck and neck as they entered the town. Mike, ever the showman, waited until he was in front of the crowds at Parliament Square before passing Read and going on to take victory.

Climbing out of Ramsey we negotiate the famous hairpin bend, which forces riders to slow before accelerating again. On the Isle of Man this is a natural feature, but it has been replicated on almost every purpose-built racing circuit in the world. Soon we pass the 26th milestone, now renamed 'Joey's' in honour of the late Joey Dunlop of Balleymoney, Northern Ireland. In his later years Dunlop was a Honda factory rider and notched up an incredible twenty-six TT wins in the course of his career, a tally which is yet to be beaten.

This is followed by the Guthrie memorial, a stone cairn surmounted by a single broken column. It marks the spot where Hawick's Jimmy Guthrie (a six-time TT winner and one of the biggest names in racing in the 1930s)

The memorial to Jimmy Guthrie, at the point at which he retired during his final TT, in 1937

broke down in his last ever TT, the 1937 Senior. A few weeks later Guthrie was killed while competing in the 1937 German Grand Prix. Conspiracy theorists claim that delays in getting medical treatment for Guthrie contributed to his death and were a deliberate Nazi ploy to remove a rival at a time when they were trying to achieve their ambition of dominating international motorcycle racing.

The Mountain Mile is a steeply climbing section, which places great demands on machinery. It leads us to the sweeping section known as the Veranda. Here, the four bends give commanding views out over the Laxey valley. On your right, you will pass the angular shape of the Les Graham Memorial, a marshal's shelter which is oddly reminiscent of the Sydney Opera House! In fact the design is inspired by an Italian alpine shepherd's hut, because the funding for it in part came from Graham's team, the Italian firm of MV Agusta. Les Graham was a former Lancaster bomber pilot and DFC holder who was 500cc world champion in 1949. He was killed in a crash at the 1953 TT.

As you approach the last bend and prepare to cross the tram tracks at the level crossing, a large building comes into view high on the right. This was built in the 1950s as as a Cold War listening station, intended to pick up the telltale signs of a Soviet missile launch. Outbuildings contained generators, and underfloor storage for food and water would have allowed the occupants to be self sufficient. With improvements in radar and other technology, it became redundant and in its later years it became famous as Murray's Motorcycle Museum. Though the museum has since closed, a sculpture of Joey Dunlop still stands outside and is a popular place of pilgrimage for TT fans.

Shortly we come to Hailwood's Height, the highest point on the TT course at 1,385ft. This section was named after Mike Hailwood, one of the greatest names in British motorsport. His dramatic TT comeback is still talked about today, and breathed new life into the event at a time when it was struggling to survive. Further on, we find Duke's bend, named in honour of Geoff Duke. A motorcycling superstar in the 1950s, he was a World Champion as well as six-times TT winner.

The origins of Windy Corner are fairly self explanatory once one has been up there, but the name Keppel Gate is perhaps more obscure. It reflects the fact that there were once sheep gates across the road which riders in early morning practice had to stop and open! The gates were not removed permanently until 1934. An old stone gatepost may, in fact, still be seen next to the marshals' hut at this point. Riders need to scrub off a lot of speed as they come to this point, and heavy braking is required before Keppel Gate.

New Zealand TT rider Bruce Anstey roars off the Mountain. In the distance, at the top of the straight stands Kate's Cottage. (Courtesy of TT Press office)

Coming down off the mountain now, we pass on the right Kate's Cottage, a solidly built white house. The building was once home to a shepherd named Tate, who worked on the hillsides. However, Graham Walker (father of Formula 1 commentator Murray Walker) who covered the TT for the BBC in the 1930s misheard the name, and described it in his radio broadcasts as Kate's Cottage. The new name stuck, and the house has subsequently become a famous landmark. Two long straights now take us back down towards Douglas, with a bend between the two at the Creg ny Baa. This hostelry is again famous with TT fans, and its walls are adorned with pictures of racers. As well as good food and beer, and excellent vantage points, it has the added bonus of being easily accessible when racing is on via the back road from Laxey. After the second straight we reach Brandish Corner, named after Walter Brandish who crashed in the right-hand gutter at this point and broke a leg while trying to pass another competitor during practice for the 1923 TT races.

Passing Cronk ny Mona we soon reach Signpost Corner, a sharp right-hander which takes us down under the pedestrian footbridge at Hailwood Avenue. To date, Mike Hailwood is the only TT competitor to have the

The Creg ny Baa, one of many pubs and hotels which line the historic TT course. (Courtesy of TT press office)

honour of a road named after him, another mark of the respect in which he is held on the Isle of Man. This bend is also known as Bedstead Corner, so named from the fact that it was common practice for Manx farmers in years gone by to fill gaps in their hedges with parts of old bed frames, as was once the case here. The bend might seem innocuous enough at 30mph in a car, but for racers it can be challenging and more than a few have been caught out here. At the bottom of the road the course follows Governor's Dip, the old road no longer used as a public highway. As the riders slow right down to negotiate the tricky bend at the bottom, which is often made more hazardous by green algae from the shadow of the trees, this again is a popular spot for photography.

Finally, the riders approach the grandstand along the Glencrutchery Road straight. This is a spot made famous by '60s and '70s commentator Peter Kneale (Manx born and bred and a TT expert, but also a regular reporter

TT Motorcycles lined up under a race team awning, during a paddock walkabout

for BBC TV's Grandstand on motorcycle racing in general). Kneale would often claim from the commentary box to be able to make out individual riders as they approached the finish line, and his catch phrase 'I can see the sun glinting on the fairing', has gone down in TT folklore.

After a race or practice session, riders and machines return to the paddock behind the grandstand, to debrief or perhaps make alterations. Here again, the TT remains true to its roots because unlike many other similar motorsport events, at certain times the paddock is accessible to fans. They can walk between the awnings to get a closer look at the machines which earlier have circulated at phenomenal speeds. Merchandise is often available to buy, and who knows, you may even spot a personal hero and perhaps get an autograph or two.

CHAPTER 6

Wartime and the Swinging Sixties

The thriving holiday trade on the Isle of Man would be interrupted twice by war in the twentieth century. On both occasions, the Island was deeply affected by the conflict, and much of its infrastructure turned over to war purposes. Afterwards, it bounced back again as the premier playground of the working and middle classes – if not of Britain as a whole, then certainly of the northwest. It was not until the close of the swinging sixties and the beginning of the '70s that the sun finally set on this holiday paradise.

It is perhaps surprising, given the enormous impact which the First World War had upon the Isle of Man, that there is not more evidence of it to be seen. The only surviving substantial structure is the former drill hall on Peel Road. Unlike most parts of the United Kingdom, the Island's armed forces were not governed by the Act of Parliament which had established the Territorial Force, and it remained the only locality still to have a volunteer formation (the 7th (Isle of Man) Volunteer Battalion) based at the drill hall. Upon the outbreak of war in 1914 this unit was not immediately mobilised for overseas service, but instead was under the command of the Lieutenant Governor, and was used to guard vital and vulnerable places on the Island.

However, the Isle of Man was to play an unexpected role in this unfolding conflict. As early as September 1914 the British government, concerned by growing spy hysteria, began to arrest German and Austro-Hungarian civilians living in Britain. The idea that civilians could be partisan and needed to be controlled, had first taken hold during the Boer War, when the first concentration camps were established. Now these potentially hostile enemy civilians were initially collected into transit camps. Somewhere more secure was required, however, and the Cunningham's Holiday Camp for young men on the Island seemed to offer the ideal solution. No sooner had the last holidaymakers left, than the first enemy aliens began to arrive.

Initially there was a holiday atmosphere as the Germans and Austrians enjoyed the last of the summer weather under canvas. As more and more arrived, however, overcrowding became a serious issue. Problems with the quality of the food also impacted on the mood of the camp and in November 1914 there was a riot in which the guards opened fire. Five internees were killed, and these were the only shots fired in anger on the Isle of Man during the entire conflict. The camp remained in operation throughout the war, though today the site is sadly lost under the carpark of the Shoprite supermarket, on Victoria Road.

The realisation that the war would not be over by Christmas spurred the search for a location for a purpose-built camp and in 1915 Knockaloe, near Peel, opened its gates. This would become the largest internment camp anywhere in the world, and at its peak held some 26,000 Germans, Austro-Hungarians and Ottoman citizens. It was so large that it required its own railway line, a spur from St John's, to be constructed in order to bring in supplies. In reality it was four camps under one central command, and the men who were to make this their home for up to five years organised an elaborate structure of educational classes, craft workshops and sporting leagues, as well as gardening clubs and theatre companies.

In 1932 Paul Cohen-Portheim published his memoir of Knockaloe, *Time Stood Still*. His view of the camp was more benign, but he acknowledged that much of this was down to his personal outlook. He wrote of his arrival there in the dead of night:

> The chains of light came nearer and nearer ... Barbed wire appeared, long, endlessly long stretches of barbed wire, five or six yards high. And faces and faces behind the wire, thousands of caged animals. They called out to us, and as in a nightmare they repeated the cries of the East End crowd: 'Huns! Baby-killers! Have they caught you at last!' This was not meant unkindly, but the form of humour peculiar to prisoners was as yet unknown to me, also I was very, very weary. At last a gate opened in the barbed wire wall, we entered, one's feet sank deep into slippery clay. In front of us lay on the left free space, on the right tightly-clustered wooden huts, the whole surrounded by tall barbed

wire and arc-lamps. This was called a compound; it held one thousand human animals. Five compounds formed a camp, and this was Camp II. There were five camps altogether, I believe. The gate closed behind us. This, then, was 'the second camp,' the disc had been delivered, there was nothing more to be done but wait for liberation – which already seemed much, much farther than twenty-four hours ago in Stratford – or else for the end of the Great War.

First impressions are by no means always right but they are frequently decisive. My first impression of Stratford had been sickening; my first impression on seeing Knockaloe Camp in daylight was one of delighted surprise, brought about, no doubt, by the contrast with the scene that had met my eyes the previous morning. Stepping out of the hut I found radiant sunshine, marvellously pure and bracing air, and a panorama of turf clad hills. That is how, in spite of all that was to follow, Knockaloe has remained in my mind, for I am what the French call a type visuel, which means that the look of a thing, place, or person matters most to me. When choosing a house or flat I have always been apt to consider the view from the window more important than more practical matters, and if I had to choose an internment camp – which I hope to God I shall never have to again – I should be guided by similar considerations. This is apt to annoy other people a good deal. Knockaloe was considered the most distasteful of all camps, the one where hardships were worst and conditions most unpleasant, that is why I feel apologetic to my fellow-prisoners when I state that I rather liked being there. It is only fair, however, to add that my stay there was short and that we had marvellous summer weather. The case of the men who were there for years ... is, of course, a very different one.

His induction consisted of a speech from the commandant, translated afterwards into German:

And that ended the ceremony. And now, what next? Now there was nothing to do, nothing at all, nothing whatsoever, nothing – for how long?[22]

At the end of the war, the site was cleared and the thousands of wooden huts of which it had been comprised were sold off. Today the land belongs to the Isle of Man government, having been for a long time the Island's experimental farm. It is possible to visit Knockaloe today, though beyond the stone engine shed which housed the locomotive, and the brick-built meat warehouses, there is nothing much to see. As you leave or arrive, look carefully at the dry stone walls lining the path. They are made up of thousands of pieces of broken concrete – all that remains of the bases of the huts.

Before leaving the area, it is worth visiting Patrick churchyard, almost directly opposite the camp entrance. Here, both guards and inmates who died during the war were laid to rest. The former are identified by the standard Commonwealth War Graves headstones. Most of the latter however were removed in the 1960s to the large German war cemetery at Cannock Chase in Staffordshire. The site of their graves is represented by the large open rectangular plot behind the church. Now the only remaining graves are those of some Ottoman prisoners, and of two Jewish internees whose family objected to their proposed re-interment alongside SS graves at Cannock, and who asked for them to remain undisturbed. Note the stones left by visitors on the headstones, according to Jewish tradition. A visitor centre has also recently opened in the adjacent Patrick schoolrooms.

Between the wars the Island once again became Britain's premier holiday resort. In this era the most popular mode of transport for tourists was the charabanc – many thousands of war-surplus lorries had become available and numbers of these were converted on the Isle of Man into open topped buses (or 'charas'). The drivers would often take Douglas holidaymakers south to **Rushen Abbey** for dancing or strawberry and cream teas. The former monastery had been subsequently used as a school, but by the twentieth century it had been reinvented as a pleasure garden. It was said that many couples owed their marriages to a meeting on the dance floor there, blissfully unaware that as their eyes met and they sashayed to the sound of the music, under their feet lay the bones of hundreds of monks, buried within the walls of the monastery. Today the site is open to the public during the summer months, operated by Manx National Heritage. The interpretation and visitor centre explores both the medieval and modern aspects of its history, while outside the extensive grounds offer a chance for a pleasant stroll along the lines of the ancient walls, the stone long-since robbed and their traces now only visible courtesy of gravel.

Florrie Forde, the music hall performer who made her home on the Isle of Man in the summer months

As the charabancs headed towards the abbey, they passed over the **Fairy Bridge** and visitors were encouraged to say hello to 'themselves', as the fairies were known. Manx folklore is unusually resilient and many customs and beliefs rooted in Celtic tradition survived into the twentieth century. In this particular case, however, the drivers had transplanted a story originally associated with a much smaller bridge, situated some distance from the main road. The custom of saying hello to the fairies continues and many modern visitors leave notes and other items for them.

In the inter-war era the theatres of Douglas attracted the best in British music-hall talent. Florrie Forde, the famous Australian singer had a holiday home at **Niarbyl** and would perform summer seasons on the Island. Her most famous song was *Has Anybody Here Seen Kelly,* originally titled *Kelly From the Isle of Man.* In later years Florrie Forde had her own review show which featured many of the up-and-coming acts of the era. As mentioned earlier, most of the big touring summer shows started on the Isle of Man before moving on to other seaside resorts. Some of the biggest names in comedy appeared on the Isle of Man, including Nat Jackley, who would go on to top the bill at the Royal Variety Performance; Wilson, Keppel and Betty, who were famous for the Sand Dance, and Jack Edge, a Liverpool comic with a reputation for blue jokes. Harry Korris, who became nationally famous as a radio comedian, was born in Douglas and began his career there. Undoubtedly the most famous star to be associated with the Isle of Man in this era was George Formby, thanks to his 1936 film *No Limit* set at the TT races; it was an instant hit and has been re-released several times. A statue of George Formby in 1930s racing gear, along with his trademark ukulele, can be found outside **Douglas Town Hall**.

During the Second World War the Island became an armed camp. In addition to providing accommodation to enemy aliens once again, it played host to hundreds of army, navy and RAF personnel under training, and by the war's end boasted three operational airfields. Unlike the situation in the First World War, no purpose-built camps were constructed. Instead, large blocks of hotels and guesthouses were requisitioned, with the authorities erecting barbed-wire compounds around them to provide security. Several were situated on Douglas seafront, but these have suffered heavily from post-war redevelopment, and many of the original wartime hotels have been demolished. The best preserved internment camp in Douglas is **Hutchinson Square**, which survives largely intact, while in Onchan, the houses which were requisitioned at Port Jack are still mostly present. Even so, a considerable amount of imagination is required to visualise these areas under wartime conditions. For those who had a relative interned on the Isle of Man, a visit to the site of their incarceration can be an emotional experience, though it is often frustratingly difficult to pinpoint precisely which house a forebear was held in.

Hutchinson Camp was regarded as the 'University' of the Isle of Man, as so many noted intellectuals and artists were incarcerated there. Probably the most significant of the artists was Kurt Schwitters, the avant-garde pioneer of Mertz. Like many German artists of the 1930s his work fell foul of the Nazis, and he was forced to flee his homeland.

Kurt Schwitters, the avant garde German artist who fled from the Nazis because his work was not suitably Aryan. He was confined as an enemy alien in Hutchinson Camp

While in Hutchinson Camp he made collages from scrap materials brought to him by other prisoners, and sculptures made from porridge, the only material available, which eventually went mouldy. Today, Schwitters is regarded as one of the most important German artists of the twentieth century. Another creative or artistic product of Hutchinson Camp was the Amadeus Quartet, a group of emigre Jewish violinists, the principal members of which had met while interned there.

During the early part of the war, a number of ships from the Isle of Man Steam Packet Company were chartered for troop carrying duties. With the collapse of France and the evacuation of British forces from Dunkirk in May 1940, many of these ships were pressed into service to assist with the rescue. Indeed it is a popular misconception (deliberately fostered by Winston Churchill) that the bulk of the British Army was brought home in the 'little ships'. In fact only the Merchant Navy had the lifting capacity to effect an evacuation of this nature and the IoMSPCo was one of the largest contributors of ships. It could even be argued that the part it played at Dunkirk was the Isle of Man's greatest contribution to victory. This assistance did not come without considerable cost, however, and three of the company's ships were lost on the same day, with great loss of life.

In 2010 the wreck of one of these ships, *Mona's Queen* III, was located by French divers, and one of her anchors was raised, with the objective of returning it to the Isle of Man as a memorial. The anchor was unveiled on 29 May 2012, the anniversary of the sinking, and the **Mona's Queen Anchor** at Kallow point now forms the centrepiece of a memorial to all of the IoMSPCo crewmen who lost their lives at Dunkirk.

With the fall of France, western Britain now became vulnerable to air attack from German planes operating from captured French bases. The Isle of Man took on renewed importance in providing early warning against aircraft coming up the Irish Sea (using the lights and radio signals of Dublin for guidance) to attack Liverpool, Glasgow and Belfast. Several radar stations were established as part of the Chain Home and Chain Home Low networks. That in the south of the Island, at Cregneash, is largely on public land and is readily accessible, though little remains above ground level apart from pillboxes, so a lot of imagination (and a plan of the site) are required. At Scarlett near Castletown, the remains of barrack blocks and

The Isle of Man Steam Packet steamer Mona's Queen, *sinking after striking a mine outside Dunkirk, on 29 May 1940. (Imperial War Museum)*

operations buildings are more extensive, while the buildings of the **Niarbyl** radar station in the west are on private farmland but may be seen from the road. Many rumours surrounded radar during the war, and indeed so secret was it that many of those involved remained silent about it for the remainder of their lives. One particular rumour concerning Niarbyl had it that the station contained special equipment for blocking the signal of Radio Eireann from Dublin (which the German bombers were using for navigation) or for bouncing it back in order to confuse them.

A good account of life at RAF Scarlett in January of 1942 comes from an American named James S. Farrior who was posted there. Farrior was from Alabama and although he wore RAF style uniform, he was in fact a member of the Civilian Technical Corps (CTC). The members of this formation were recruited throughout the USA from university students with a knowledge of physics, radio station technicians and others of a similar bent, in order to provide the specialist staff to man the expanding Chain Home system. Farrior kept a fascinating diary of his experiences on the Isle of Man, and it records the sense of wonder with which this young man from the Deep South encountered the winding streets of Castletown, and the ancient headstones in churchyards. He also records that the main form of entertainment for airmen and soldiers based around Castletown was a visit to the Cosy Cinema, where the cigarette smoke in the small auditorium was so thick during a performance that it burned his eyes.

RAF Scarlett had four 325ft steel, guyed towers which supported the two sets of transmitting curtain arrays (Main and Standby). There were also two 240ft self-supporting towers made of wood. These supported the receiving dipoles and had to be climbed at regular intervals for inspection, not a job for the faint-hearted. In February of that year, maintenance was required upon one of the curtain arrays and although it did not require climbing, it was still a tedious job. Farrior writes:

> This morning, despite the cold, damp, windy weather, we had to take down the curtain array from the 325 foot towers near T Block-1 to make a repair and to clean the insulators. Letting it down with the winch was a slow process, and after it was down, we had to spread it out on the ground so we could work on it. The towers are located near the edge of the sea, and the cold wind was blowing directly off the sea. It was a miserable day of work.
>
> We got the array down, made the repair, and cleaned the insulators. Putting it back up was not easy, as everything had to be kept untangled as the array was cranked back up. When it was finally back in place, we examined it with a telescope and found to our dismay that some of the open wire feeders had become twisted. That meant that it must come down again. The work had not been finished when I got off at 5pm.
>
> We have a standby transmitter block, T Block-2, which has an identical MB2 transmitter and curtain array that we use when the main one is being repaired. In a field to the east of the transmitting towers used with T Block 2, is a dummy (decoy) transmitter block. It is not actually a block, but is something made to look like a poorly camouflaged block. Sometimes, when an inexperienced radio mechanic arrives at Scarlett, the location of the dummy block is pointed out, and he is directed to 'go there and assist the mechanic who is repairing the

dummy MB2 transmitter.' If he is a 'dummy' radio mechanic, he will go there before he realizes that it is a joke.[23]

RAF Scarlett would eventually be closed due to the expansion of the airfield at Ronaldsway, because its 325ft aerial masts were well inside the mandatory 6,000 yard construction limit. The station was mothballed shortly after the completion later in 1942 of a new facility, RAF Dalby at Niarbyl, though both ran simultaneously for a time to ensure unbroken cover.

Looking south towards the wartime radar masts at Niarbyl. The steel masts in the foreground stood some 300 feet tall. The shorter masts closer to the shore were wooden decoys. (Courtesy of John Hall)

As well as radar sites the RAF also operated three airfields on the Island. RAF Ronaldsway, the former civilian airfield, was mainly used for training, but RAF Jurby and RAF Andreas in the north were home to various operational fighter squadrons which provided air cover over the Irish Sea, in particular the approaches to Liverpool. Although RAF Jurby had been planned as a training station, and its first unit was No 5 Air Observers School, life here was soon about more than just practice. Some active fighter squadrons arrived at Jurby in the autumn of 1940, starting with the Boulton Paul Defiants of No. 307 Squadron. These turret-armed fighters were followed by three Hawker Hurricane squadrons (Nos. 258, 302 and 312) and later the Supermarine Spitfires of No. 457 Squadron for convoy patrol sorties, which were highly important duties. Later in the war Jurby was home to second-line bomber squadrons operating Handley Page Hampdens, but even these were pressed into service on some of the '1,000 bomber raids' when every aircraft the RAF had available and airworthy was thrown into action. By the end of May 1945 the resident instructional unit at Jurby had changed name, to become known as No. 5 Air Navigation School, but life for those in training carried on largely as before, with occasional visits to the bright lights of Douglas breaking the monotony. Training equipment had also changed, with Avro Ansons and Vickers Wellingtons now making up the bulk. RAF Jurby continued in use until the 1960s.

The runways of both Jurby and Andreas are still extant, and in both cases many of the airfield buildings have been turned over to light industrial use. The control towers of both airfields may still be seen, and in the graveyard of Jurby church may be found the familiar Commonwealth War Graves headstones of those who died here, mainly in accidents. Notable among these are the headstones of Polish and Czech aircrew who trained on the Island.

Later in the war the RAF handed Ronaldsway to the Royal Navy, which undertook major redevelopment of the site. Among other infrastructure improvements came hard runways and additional hangars. Many of these items are still evident today, and as an incidental point, the extension work revealed more of the archaeological evidence which was already known to exist at Ronaldsway, and established beyond all doubt that the Neolithic culture which had existed on the Island was unique.

Unlike most airfields constructed during the Second World War (including Andreas), which conformed to the standard RAF three-runway pattern, Ronaldsway had four runways to comply with admiralty requirements – crosswinds were not a problem on aircraft carriers and so there had to be more choices of 'into wind' runway. The runways were also narrower than the standard 50 yards, because in order to simulate aircraft-carrier deck-landings they were only 30 yards wide. Post war this would result in considerable work to widen two of them to civil aviation standards. HMS *Urley*, as the the base was known, came into being officially on 21 June 1944 and had as its main task torpedo-bomber reconnaissance and associated training. The first Fleet Air Arm unit, 747 Naval Air Squadron, arrived on 14 July 1944 equipped with Fairey Barracuda II aircraft, followed by 713 Naval Air Squadron on 12 August, also with Barracuda IIs. The final Barracuda squadron, 710 Naval Air Squadron, reformed at Ronaldsway on 7 October. It was equipped with Barracuda II and III aeroplanes, and also operated the Fairey Swordfish biplane. The three permanently based squadrons had ninety-two Barracudas between them, out of a total of 120 naval aircraft based at Ronaldsway. There were also several temporary detachments of squadrons to HMS *Urley*, including four Miles Martinets from 725 Naval Air Squadron based there between August and November to provide Air-to-Air firing facilities. There are several memorials to units based at Ronaldsway within the terminal building.

Today a number of original wartime buildings may also still be seen at the airport, though most are not accessible. However the former photographic development building now forms the home of the **Manx Aviation and Military Museum**, an institution run entirely by local volunteers which provides a home for a number of relics from wartime crashes in this area, as well as wider information on the Island's wartime role. The museum also houses the collection of the Manx Regiment Old Comrades Association. The regiment was raised in 1938 as Britain desperately rearmed, and was officially the 15th Light Anti-Aircraft Regiment Royal Artillery.

As the war progressed many of the inhabitants of the internment camps were, after tribunal hearings, found to offer no threat to national security and were released. The accommodation which subsequently became available was often taken over by the armed forces for training purposes.

Granville Camp on Douglas seafront in this way became HMS *Valkyrie*, a shore establishment for the training of Royal Navy radar technicians. The most famous resident of HMS *Valkyrie* was undoubtedly the actor Jon Pertwee, later to become a household name as Dr Who on television. As a 22 year old naval lieutenant, however, he was at the start of his acting career, and the Isle of Man provided him with many opportunities to develop his talent. He wrote afterwards that the beautiful Gaiety theatre, just a stone's throw from his accommodation, was his inspiration to form a company of local amateurs and servicemen, among whom there were a number of professionals:

> My first production for 'The Service Players', as the company came to be known, was Night Must Fall by Emlyn Williams ... as I had always wanted to play Danny. But as my Welsh accent was not of the best quality, I decided to play it in Cockney and it seemed to work. The following 'critique' was to me no ordinary one, written as it was by the ex-editor of *The Yorkshire Post*, Mr George Brown. As such it gave me tremendous heart and encouragement at that time, and also during the ensuing years. Of my performance as Danny, in Night Must Fall, Mr Brown said:-

> Danny, played by a Sub-Lieutenant in the RNVR named Pertwee was really magnificent. Having seen the play in London, and having seen it on the films, we would give Mr Pertwee's portrayal of Danny as the best of them. He has before him a fine future on the English stage.

> My co-producer was Sub-Lieutenant Jack Williams RNVR, now a most eminent television director. Among the cast was one professional opera singer, Norah Moore, and one professional actor, an old friend, Kenneth Henry, who played Inspector Belsize. Mrs Bramson was played by Olga Cowell, the wife of a respected lawyer in Douglas, Robert Cowell, who was also the Steward of the Isle of Man TT. This magnificent grande dame, for she could only be so described, could wipe the floor with 95 per cent of all the professional character actresses I have seen. She was in the Dame May Whitty/Margaret Rutherford mould, and with her grace and impeccable timing was a joy to work with. A tall, statuesque, bosomy lady, she carried herself with tremendous dignity

and, like many large people, her feet positively twinkled. A turn around the dance floor with Olga was an experience not to be missed. She also played the piano with great flair and skill, a rare talent that I shamelessly tried to include into whatever play we were doing at the time. For many years I tried to persuade Olga Cowell to turn professional, but she would have none of it. 'Nonsense dear, I'm just a second rate amateur, no one would ever employ me,' she said. In every play we presented she received notices from the critics that should have convinced her otherwise, but she was adamant and stayed an amateur ...[24]

The most decorated Manx soldier of the Second World War was Major Robert Henry Cain, born in Shanghai but of Manx parents. He returned to the Island to be educated at King William's College near Castletown, and in his later years also retired to the Island. Cain was awarded the Victoria Cross while serving with an airborne battalion of the South Staffordshire Regiment during the Battle of Arnhem. He repeatedly placed himself in danger by attempting to destroy enemy tanks while armed with a PIAT, and was wounded during the battle. In recent years a crossing over the harbour in Castletown has been named the Cain Bridge in honour of him.

With the close of hostilities in 1945, the Island's tourist industry began to prepare for the return of paying guests. The immediate post-war years would see British industrial workers with money in their pockets, but little to spend it on during a period of austerity. Foreign travel was also almost impossible in this era, and so the Isle of Man was well placed to provide holidays. Among those who came to the Island was band leader Hugh Gibb, who had a residency at the Douglas Bay Hotel among other establishments. Three of Hugh's children were born on the Isle of Man in subsequent years – Maurice, Robin and Sir Barry Gibb, who would go on to form one of the most successful British vocal groups of all time, the Bee Gees. The Gibbs' childhood home, **50 St Catherine's Drive**, Douglas now features a blue plaque, commemorating its association, as does Union Mills post office, which was run by the family. Maurice Gibb in particular retained a connection with the Island until the band reached superstar status in the late 1970s, owning a large house in Douglas, playing snooker at the Douglas Snooker hall and even marshalling at the TT races.

The one time home of the Gibb brothers, who would later form the Bee Gees pop group

This, however, was not the Island's only famous musical association. In the 1950s – before they knew each other – both John Lennon and Paul McCartney holidayed on the Isle of Man; McCartney later designed a set of Manx stamps reflecting his happy childhood memories. Pete Townshend of The Who also spent much time on the Island while his father was a musician with the Squadronaires, the former RAF big band which performed every night at the Palace Ballroom in the 1950s.

In this decade the Island's most notorious resident was undoubtedly Gerald Brousseau Gardner, credited as the father of modern witchcraft or paganism. Gardner was an associate and friend of Aleister Crowley, famous as a proponent of black magic and Satanism, and created a stir in post-war Britain when, following the repeal of the Witchcraft Act, he published several books describing the Wicca religion, such as *High Magic's Aid* (1949) and *Witchcraft Today* (1954). Gardner claimed it was the ancient religion of the British Isles, which had been driven almost to extinction by the persecution of the 1600s. Despite the fact that Gardner made most of it up as he went along, today Wicca is one of the fastest growing religions in the world. Gardner, together with another associate, Cecil Williamson founded the Museum of Witchcraft at the **Witches Mill** in Castletown. Later Gardner ran it alone. He created an entirely fictitious history for the disused windmill, and claimed it had been used by seventeenth-century witches even though it was unquestionably of much later date. The mill and surrounding buildings are now in private ownership, though it may be seen from Arbory Road.

Gerald Gardner at work in his Museum of Witchcraft, in the 1950s

The Island's post-war resurgence as a holiday destination proved to be something of a faltering affair. Much of its tourist accommodation had been damaged during the war, and as visitor expectations increased, many of the smaller proprietors would struggle to upgrade their properties in line with them. Nevertheless, as the Swinging Sixties dawned the Island tried to position itself ahead of rival resorts and passed legislation to legalise gambling, in advance of the United Kingdom. The Palace casino, which opened in 1964, was among the first in Britain and was launched by the actor Sean Connery. At the time, Connery (who was starring as James Bond) was just about the most famous British actor in the world. The same year, the Victorian Derby Castle was demolished to make way for **Summerland**, the new all-weather holiday centre. Sadly, this visionary structure which might have prolonged the Island's life as a holiday destination was doomed by faulty construction methods, and was destroyed in a devastating fire in 1974. A memorial to the victims of the fire now stands at the northern end of the Promenade close to the site.

Another building which survives from the brief 1960s tourism revival is the distinctive and futuristic-looking new **Sea Terminal** in Douglas, which was opened by Princess Margaret. First planned in 1956, the building took around four years to complete, the work being done mainly in the winter months. It was intended to replace the Victorian structure which had stood on this site with something resembling an airport departure lounge. The design incorporates the three legs of man, dividing the pier into three distinct zones: a covered waiting area which was the first part to be completed, in 1962; a dockside reception area where horse trams and foot passengers would arrive, and a new entrance with parking for six double-decker buses. A continuous canopy linked a covered walkway to the King Edward pier (incidentally the only public structure in Britain to be named after King Edward VIII) from the promenade. Above it all was the Crow's Nest restaurant (long since converted into offices), the serrated roof and central spire of which gave rise to the building's nickname: 'the lemon squeezer'. In 2014 a proposal to sweep away the Sea Terminal in favour of a deep water berth for cruise ships aroused a campaign to save it. Built at an important turning point in Manx history, it is one of the few twentieth-century buildings of quality on the Island, and is held in great esteem by many.

Douglas remained a major entertainment venue. The Rolling Stones played at the Palace in 1964, while other bands such as Freddie and the Dreamers held summer-long residencies. The Island's greatest claim to fame in this era however was through its association with Radio Caroline. The station purportedly got its name when the founder Ronan O'Rahily saw a photo of President Kennedy's daughter Caroline playing in the Oval Office, and holding up the entire machinery of government. It was an image and an idea that he liked, and Radio Caroline is credited with kickstarting the 'Swinging Sixties'. At the time pop music was strictly rationed. The BBC played only one hour a week, and there was no independent radio. Interestingly, Britain had commercial TV before she had commercial radio – the powerful propaganda value of 'wireless' in wartime was a memory that lived long in government circles, and while television was considered a trivial, if entertaining, diversion, radio was thought to be too important to be outside of official control.

Undoubtedly the most famous off-shore pirate radio station of them all, Caroline challenged the establishment head-on, broadcasting round-the-clock pop music to an eager audience of teenagers, and it only came to an end when the government of Harold Wilson changed the law by introducing the Marine Offences Act. In the process it created BBC Radio 1, the new station hoovering up the best of the pirate DJs. The northern ship arrived in Manx waters on Tynwald Day 1964 and, renamed MV *Caroline,* she would broadcast to northern England, Scotland and Ireland for four years. Pop acts were equally eager for the exposure pirate radio could offer, and were keen to be associated with Caroline. Freddie and the Dreamers were just one of the headliners of the day who were photographed aboard the ship.

The Manx town with the strongest connection to Radio Caroline is undeniably Ramsey, from whence tender vessels would depart carrying supplies, crew members and VIP visitors out to the ship. Fans (and radio hams) would also try to hitch a ride on a supply boat, or indeed any fishing vessel that would take them out close enough to get a good view of the legendary ship. The disparaging term that the DJs had for these sightseers in their wet-weather gear – the 'anoraks' – has come down to us today. A visit to 'Caroline Corner' in Ramsey is a must for anyone who remembers those heady – if innocent – days. The station's onshore office, 'PO Box 3 Ramsey', became one of the most famous addresses in the British Isles, and the Isle of Man Post Office had to take on additional staff to handle the volume of mail it received. The Caroline office was at number 9 East Street. The DJs stayed at the Commercial Hotel (Ellan Vannin pub) on their way to and from the vessel, and through a gap in the sea wall on a clear day the ship herself, riding at anchor on the Bahama Bank, could be seen.

In the later twentieth century the Island made efforts to develop its role as a film location. The results have been varied, but perhaps the most successful movies to be filmed on the Isle of Man to date have been 1998's *Waking Ned*, when it stood in for rural Ireland – filmed mostly at Cregneash with some scenes staged at Niarbyl – and 2001's *Harry Potter and the Chamber of Secrets*. Indeed, one of the stars of that film, Geraldine Somerville, has strong family links to the Isle of Man and was brought up on the Island. In 2010, the documentary film *TT3D: Closer to the Edge* followed the exploits of racers at the TT, and is credited with making an overnight star of Guy Martin. He has since gone on to become one of the biggest names in British documentary television, presenting hugely popular programmes about engineering, racing and aviation.

The Isle of Man's links to show-business continued when popular comedy actor Sir Norman Wisdom retired to the Island. He was frequently seen at public events, and his funeral in 2010 drew large crowds. A statue of him was commissioned by Douglas Borough Council, from the Manx sculptor Amanda Barton (who also created the statue of George Formby referred to previously) which at the time of writing can be seen outside the **Sefton Hotel** (the restaurant of which is named 'Sir Norman's' in his honour). Actor

Sir Norman Wisdom, pictured at the height of his film career

John Rhys-Davies, best known for his roles in the Indiana Jones films and the Lord of the Rings trilogy, as well as for a host of TV credits, is an Island resident, while another link to the world of film came through George Macdonald Fraser. Fraser became famous as the author of the *Flashman* series of novels, which were based on the later exploits of the bully in *Tom Brown's Schooldays.* He came to live on the Island following the success of the first

Island resident George Macdonald Fraser's most memorable character was the Victorian anti-hero Flashman

novel in the series, and was also a screenwriter, with his credits including the James Bond movie *Octopussy*. Finally, well-known film critic and aficionado Mark Kermode boasts Manx ancestry and is a frequent visitor to the Island as well as patron of its annual film festival.

Thus, the Island's motto, loosely translated as 'whichever way you throw me, I will stand', is a fitting way to summarise its long and varied history. Often buffeted by winds blowing in from its larger neighbours, the Island has many times reinvented itself in order to survive, but it is a place justifiably proud of its long history. Whatever your interests, or whichever period or aspect of history captures your imagination, undoubtedly one of the myriad faces of the Isle of Man will be for you.

TOUR ROUTE 1

A Walking Tour of Douglas

Any tour of Douglas, indeed any tour of the Isle of Man, should really begin with a visit to the Manx Museum on Kingswood Grove. The headquarters and flagship of Manx National Heritage, the museum has occupied this site since 1922. Admission is free, and it provides an ideal overview of the Island's history. A short documentary film is usually available in the lecture theatre, and this gives an introduction to the main themes of Manx history. The galleries then explore various topics, including the Island's artistic heritage, the prehistoric and early Celtic inhabitants, the Vikings (be prepared for some impressive displays of silver coin hoards here), the Manx language and folklore, through to Victorian holidaymakers and the TT races. The Mann at War gallery explores the Island's military history and contains the uniform of Manx Trafalgar hero Captain John Quilliam, as well as exploring the Island's role in wartime internment. The Island's oldest surviving double-decker horse tram is on display here, as are a number of historic TT racing machines. Many of the exhibits are hands-on and interactive, and there is lots to keep children entertained, including a dedicated area called the Exploratorium. A small café serves drinks and light meals or snacks, and there is a sizable giftshop. The museum is fully accessible and also has the Island's only adult changing place.

With so much to see here it is probably worth allowing at least two hours for your visit. Although it is a good wet-weather destination, it makes sense to visit the museum as early as you can in your holiday, as a lot of what you see afterwards will then be in better context. The library and archives of Manx National Heritage are also located within this building and are a goldmine of information if, for example, you are researching Manx forebears (again, if you are planning a visit, try to fit it in earlier in your visit rather than later to give yourself more chance of success). The museum is situated at the top of Crellins Hill and can be difficult to find if you are unfamiliar with Douglas. If you are on foot, the hill itself is very steep and is best not tackled directly; use the lift on Market Street which takes you to the top of the Chester Street multi-storey car park, then cross over the pedestrian foot bridge at the northern end. If you are travelling by car, there is little parking at the museum itself, so again it is best to leave it on the multi-storey car park and use the foot bridge for access.

From the museum it is a short walk to the old part of Douglas. If you head down Crellins Hill and turn right, at the bottom, you will see the elaborate eighteenth-century Adam doorframe, which the museum rescued from the Douglas slum clearances in the 1930s. Continue along Finch Road and in about ten minutes you will pass the 'Wedding Cake', the ornate circular white building which is the home of Tynwald, the Island's parliament and the oldest continuous political assembly in the world. The 'Wedding Cake' began life as a bank and became a legislative building, unlike the Old House of Keys in Castletown, which began life as a legislative building and became a bank. The visitors' gallery is usually open to the public when sittings are in session, and details of the business of the day are posted outside. Cross over the road here, and head down Hill Street.

Directly in front of you now, across the road stands St George's church, one of the oldest and most interesting in Douglas, completed in 1781. At that time the church stood on its own, in fields on the outskirts of the town. The area around it was used during the Napoleonic Wars for drilling soldiers, and for shooting practice. On 20 February 1796, we have the following account of a review of a regiment, apparently in the field next to St George's in an ephemeral Manx newspaper entitled, *The Oracle and Public Advertiser*:

> The Royal Manx Fencibles were reviewed last Thursday in a large field near Douglas. The men fell in by companies at the High Churchyard, at 10 o'clock in the morning, dressed in their new clothing, and in half an hour after were marched to the field. General Edward Smith, accompanied by Lieut.-Colonel Taubman and his aide-de-camp Major Philpot, arrived about 11 o'clock, when he was saluted by the regiment, which was afterwards drawn up by companies in single ranks. The General then commenced his inspection, beginning with the Grenadiers, and proceeded to the other companies according to seniority,

until he closed with the light infantry. After minutely examining each man in the regiment, the General declared he had not seen a finer body of men raised during the war. He then desired to see them perform their military manœuvres, which they did with great precision, and went through the manual and platoon exercises in a manner that greatly satisfied the General, and which would have done honour to veteran corps.[25]

Much of the money raised for the construction of the church came from wealthy citizens of Douglas who had grown rich on the proceeds of the 'running trade' (smuggling), notably John Joseph Bacon. The structure is based on that of the church of St James in Whitehaven, and the trustees travelled there to inspect it before approving the design. In the days when the Earls of Derby held the Lordship of Mann, Liverpool had been the

St George's church, Douglas. The church played an important part in the Eighteenth and early Nineteenth Century life of the town

main port for the Isle of Man, but in the eighteenth century under the rule of the Dukes of Atholl this switched to Whitehaven, before reverting back to Liverpool sometime later. In this period there were strong links with Cumberland, with many Manx families having a branch or offshoot there. Among these were the Christians, whose main base was at Milntown near Ramsey, but with an offshoot at Ewanrigg, where Fletcher Christian was born. Later, after he took up residence in Douglas with his widowed mother, St George's would play a role in bringing him together with the other protagonists in the *Bounty* saga.

A walk around the churchyard is interesting. On the right of the path is the impressive tomb of Sir William Hillary, founder of the RNLI. A little further on is an open area marked by two plain wooden crosses. This is the cholera pit, a mass grave dating from the years when that disease ravaged Douglas. The church organ of St George's was the first to be installed in any church on the Isle of Man. It was made in 1741 by the renowned makers Harris & Byfield, and was acquired from the Dublin Assembly Hall in 1778 by one of the St George's Trustees, for the sum of £100 (£12,000 in 2018). It is the organ on which George Frederic Handel conducted the first performance of the Messiah, which took place in Dublin in 1742. After the organ was installed at St George's it was said that it enriched the musical life of the entire Isle of Man, with people from all over the Island making their way into Douglas to listen to it.

Leaving the churchyard, head down Upper Church Street and turn right onto Athol Street. You are now in the town's legal and financial district, though this was once a residential street, and some of the Regency-era buildings still retain their original facades. At the end on the right, we reach the site of the house once occupied by Archibald Knox, now commemorated by a garden. Directly in front now is the ornate Douglas Railway Station. The Ruabon brick gateway, with its twin gilt topped towers, was constructed in 1887. If you are planning to head south on the railway, the entrance to the station is now via a smaller gateway to the left.

Of interest here is the signal box. Built in 1892, it is located at the station throat between the carriage shed and the workshops. The Points Box, as it was called locally, contained a 36-lever frame signal box built by Dutton & Co., of Worcester, and supplied to the railway when the yard was modified

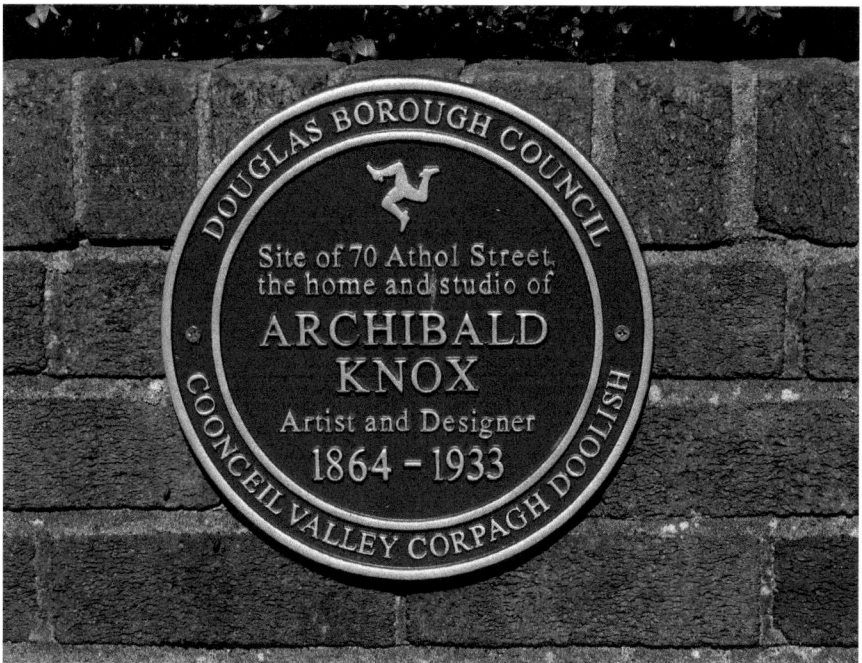

The blue plaque commemorating the residence of Archibald Knox, arguably the Island's greatest artist

and the workshops were extended. The frame is a unique survivor of the 'drink-handle' type in which the handle of the lever also serves as the catch handle. The signal box features a set of characteristic wooden external steps that must be climbed to access the levers, with storage space beneath the timber-built top section; this would have housed all the linkage and control gear. The top section also features a three-quarter glazed section and integral fireplace, and bears a considerable resemblance to Dutton's signal boxes constructed for the Great Northern Railway in Ireland about this time. From the Douglas signal box the signalman on duty had a commanding view of the entire yard, controlling every traffic movement from passenger trains to complex shunting procedures.

If you are not planning to catch a train, return along Athol Street and turn right on to Church Street. Continue until you reach a pedestrianised area.

On your left, now a restaurant, is one of the oldest buildings in Douglas, constructed in the 1780s. To your right is Barrack Street. This was once the location of a barracks built for troops stationed here during the Napoleonic Wars, though the building has long since gone. In Victorian times this was one of the worst slums in Douglas, known as Little Hell. The building with the large red door is the former fire station, in use until 1965, when the Isle of Man government took over responsibility for fire and rescue from individual boroughs. Continue down the pedestrianised section of Church Street. When you reach the pelican crossing, to your left you will see the Amanda Barton statue of George Formby, 'leaning on a lamppost', as in the words of one of his most enduring songs. George is depicted in the costume of one of his most famous characters, George Shuttleworth, the hero of *No Limit,* who comes to compete in the TT races as a complete outsider, but goes on to win and get the girl. Cross at the pelican crossing, and head down Ridgeway Street. As you pass St Matthew's church on your left, note the war memorial, designed by Archibald Knox. Continue to the harbour. You are now in the oldest part of Douglas, where antiquarians note there was once a medieval keeill site, together with lintel graves uncovered during construction works. There is also some evidence for a carved stone cross being once located here, though this has also long since gone.

Daniel King provides us with a good idea of what the south side of Douglas harbour here looked like in the aftermath of the English Civil War, as he sketched it during his tour of the Island in the 1660s. The chapel which he indicates was here in his drawing was replaced in 1708 by Old St Matthew's church, which in its turn was replaced by the Douglas Market Hall, about 150 yards or so on the left. Old St Matthews was constructed by Bishop Thomas Wilson, one of the most energetic and long-lived of Manx clergymen. Described as an 'ungainly edifice', the church nonetheless bore witness to the baptism of one of William Bligh's children, during the time that he was stationed on the Isle of Man in the 1780s, his signature clearly visible in the church register now held in the archives of the Manx Museum.

We are now standing at the heart of the Georgian town, and in the 'golden triangle' of British naval history, for just beyond the Douglas Market Hall stands the Douglas Hotel. Built by the merchant Robert Black in the heyday of the smuggling era, this imposing building was the home of Peter

The most famous event in British naval history had its origins in Douglas. It has been the subject of three Hollywood films

Heywood, another protagonist of the *Bounty* saga. Continue to the end of the row and then cut through the carpark to Lord Street. As you do so, take a look back over your shoulder, at the large white crenelated building on the far side of the harbour. This is Fort Anne, built in 1796 by Thomas 'Buck'

Whaley, a member of the Irish parliament and inveterate gambler. Among other stories and legends surrounding him, it was said that he won a wager that he could leave Ireland but still live on Irish soil. This he achieved by importing several cartloads of Irish earth which he incorporated into the foundations of the building. Later, it was the home of Sir William Hillary.

Cross at the pelican crossing on Lord Street and turn right. Continue for about 200 yards or more until you meet an unassuming lane joining Lord Street at a sharp angle from the left, just before the roundabout. This is Fort Street, named after the Tudor-era fort which once stood near the roundabout, and is one of the original streets of Georgian Douglas. Continue down Fort Street for about 100 yards. You are now at the approximate site of Fletcher Christian's house, where the young man lived with his widowed mother before embarking upon his journey into history aboard the *Bounty*.

As we continue we reach Victoria Street, the generous width of which indicates its much later date. In fact, the street was bulldozed through the twisting lanes of the old town to provide a direct link between the ferry terminal and the hotels of Upper Douglas, during the heyday of the tourist boom. Once, cable trams shuttled up and down this street, ferrying passengers to and from the waiting ships. Turn right on to Victoria Street and continue until you reach the Victoria Clock on the Promenade, a monument commemorating the 1887 Golden Jubilee. To your right you will see the distinctive shape of the 'Lemon Squeezer', the iconic Sea Terminal building designed in the 1960s, which may thus far be unfamiliar if you have travelled by air.

From this point it is possible to catch a bus or a horse tram (in summer) back along the promenade. All of the ground on which the road and hotels are built was reclaimed from the beach in the 1860s. Prior to that, the sea reached as far as Strand Street (previously known as Sand Street), and in places, sections of the impressive Georgian sea-wall with its bull-nose can still be observed behind the shops. As you travel along the promenade, bear in mind that from 1940 to 1945 many of the hotels were behind barbed wire fences, cordoned off as internment camps. In some places, the marks from the post holes can still be discerned in the tarmac of the road. Later on, many were taken over by the armed forces as training facilities, the most impressive of which was HMS *Valkyrie*, the Royal Navy's number 1 Radar Training School. On your right, you will also have a good view of the Tower of Refuge, built on the Conister Rock (otherwise known as St Mary's Isle) in Douglas Bay. On 20 November 1830 the steamer *St George* was driven on to the rock by the force of a violent gale. She had already discharged her passengers but her crew of eighteen remained on board. Seeing the difficulty she was in, Sir William Hillary at once organised a lifeboat, and despite the danger, managed to rescue all the crew without loss to his own party. A memorial to this gallant rescue can now be found on Loch Promenade. In 1832, Hillary organised the construction of the tower, as a place of safety where shipwrecked mariners could await rescue. The following year, it was the subject of a poem by the English romantic poet William Wordsworth, who was on a tour of the Isle of Man at the time.

If you leave the bus or tram somewhere just before the imposing war memorial, you are now well placed for a visit to the Gaiety Theatre, or to St Thomas' church. For the latter, head back on yourself until you pass the Sefton Hotel, then turn right, when the stone-built church comes into view. From here, it is a short walk back to the Chester Street car park.

TOUR ROUTE 2

Ramsey and the North by Car

As with the other tours in this section, it is assumed here that the visitor is staying in Douglas, though of course this itinerary may be adapted to suit a number of starting points. This suggested tour may also be adjusted or shortened to fill either half a day or a full day, depending on the length of lunch or refreshment breaks. Before planning an excursion however, note should be taken of special events such as the TT or Manx Grand Prix races which may mean certain roads are closed, or are restricted to one way traffic only. Additional traffic, which may add considerably to journey times, is also likely at these times.

Leave Douglas by means of the A2 Glencrutchery Road leading north to Onchan, and continue with the A2 towards Laxey and then Ramsey. As you leave Onchan, with the Co-op on your left, take a quick look to the right down Royal Avenue, for a view of the parish hall designed by Baillie-Scott. In the Arts and Crafts style, with sloping buttresses and roughcast walls, it was opened in 1898. After travelling through the village of Baldrine, we soon approach the mining district of Laxey. After passing the Fairy Cottage filling station on the right, take a right turn signed B1 Old Laxey. This steep and narrow road takes you down into the heart of the former mining village. As you proceed with caution down Old Laxey Hill, note the numerous picturesque cottages towards the bottom. Many would originally have been the homes of miners or those employed in other ways by the mines, and considerable numbers still retain the romantic names given to them in those days, such as Avoca. When you reach the Shore Hotel, turn right on to Tent Road. It was in this area that traditional country fairs were held, the tents in which the stallholders set out their wares is still preserved in the name. Evidence of Laxey's mining past is all around – on the right you will see the Laxey Sailing Club headquarters, once the Old Laxey Working Men's

Institute and Reading Room, opened by the miners themselves in 1871 as a means of self-improvement. At the bottom of the road we find a short breakwater and harbour, constructed by the Great Laxey Mining Company for the export of its products – lead and zinc ore.

To the right, what is now a carpark was the jack yard (black jack being a term for zinc ore) where the processed ore was marshalled for shipping, and behind that is a large three-storey stone building. This was also built by the Great Laxey Mining Company for the storage of ore, though we know it had other uses, for in the 1860s a report tells us that a social evening and dance was held on the upper floor, organised by Mrs Rowe, the wife of the Mine Captain. This was to raise funds for the Laxey Artillery Volunteers. If the weather is fine, a short walk along the promenade here offers good views of Laxey Bay. As you stroll along the seafront, over to your right is a large private house, Sea Level. Next to it, however, is the original Sea Level, a miners' cottage which in the 1890s was roofed with thatch. This was once home to the Clague family, whose story is typical of many in this area. Here in 1881 lived Henry Clague, a 34-year-old lead miner and his wife Jane, who was two years older than him. The Clagues had six children, their oldest son William, then James, a daughter Catherine, another son George, a daughter Louisa Jane and a third son Thomas Charles. In the Manx Museum's Folklife Survey are the recollections of David Boreland, a former Laxey miner, which contains more information about the times in which they lived:

> Men of my generation, when they came to 18 or 20 years of age, could find very little to do here, unless they became miners. That was why so many of them went away. £1 a week was the highest wage they could hope for here and the £4 or £5 a week that they heard reports of in the South African mines seemed wonderful to them. It was the El Dorado of those days. The passage to Cape Town didn't cost much – a man could go for £9 or £10. They used to go out in batches of ten or a dozen … with their mining experience the men from Laxey could always get a job out there … I can recall whole families of men going out. The Lawsons Robert John, Teddy and Willie, five Kewley brothers, who all died out there of Miner's Phthisis. James, George, Tommy Charles and Franklyn Clague. The first two died also.[26]

In fact Miner's Phthisis (or tuberculosis caused by dust) claimed the lives of many who went to South Africa, and it was said that the only ones who made real money from the South African goldfields were the man who sold the miners their passage, and the undertaker who buried them.

Leaving the harbour, retrace your steps towards the Shore Hotel and turn right over the bridge. This structure is the modern replacement of a bridge which washed away in a violent storm in 2014. When branches and other debris accumulated in the arches, torrents of water from the river swollen by unprecedented rain destroyed the carriageway, tipping a double-decker bus into the river in the process. Fortunately no lives were lost, and in the subsequent reconstruction work, the remains of the earlier eighteenth-century pack-horse bridge were found at the core of the old structure. This was where the original road from Ramsey to Douglas crossed the Laxey River, and in those days, before mining became a boom industry, linen was the chief commodity of the district. Illustrations from the 1790s show it laid out to be bleached along the river bank here.

Continue along Glen Road, passing the imposing former Wesleyan Methodist chapel with its date stone of 1850 on your left. Laxey was a stronghold of Methodism, with strong Wesleyan and Primitive congregations. Further on, on the right-hand side of the road we come to Laxey Woollen Mills. This institution started life as a water-powered corn mill but was acquired by Egbert Rydings, a silk weaver from Clitheroe in Lancashire and the St George's Guild founded by John Ruskin, which sought to promote traditional crafts and industries. It reopened as such in 1881. The mills operated on the principle, 'from the mountain track to the wearer's back' – i.e. you should be able to have a suit made out of the wool you supplied to the mill. The use of steam-powered machinery was not allowed, but was briefly introduced in the 1940s and 1950s, until the mills returned to hand production as today. The Manx tartan is one of its most popular products.

From here we bear left over the river once more and continue towards the impressive crenelated viaduct of the Manx Electric Railway. Passing underneath, at the top of Church Hill we rejoin the A2 heading right. Shortly the Mines Tavern comes into view. This was formerly the home of Mine Captain Richard Rowe, who presided over the most prosperous era in the history of the Laxey Mine, the 1850s. Later, with the construction of the

MER part of the house was demolished to make way for the tracks which run adjacent to it. Passing over the level crossing we see the dark green of the MER shed on the right, and on the left, the tracks of the Snaefell Mountain Railway. As we approach the bend in the road, take the left turn once more across the railway tracks towards the Great Laxey Wheel. As you do so take a glance at the building on the corner now behind us – it has a grim history, being used as a temporary mortuary for those killed in the Snaefell Mine Disaster of 1897, further up the valley. This was the worst mining disaster in the Island's history, when a candle accidentally started an underground fire, which in turn led to a build up of carbon monoxide. When the next shift descended, nineteen men were fatally overcome by toxic fumes.

Laxey Wheel is by now visible in the distance, an imposing industrial monument, dominating the landscape. The three legs symbol on the stonework is a powerful statement on the part of the builder of the Wheel, the banker and industrialist George W. Dumbell. Just on our left is a statue of a miner, unveiled in 2015 to commemorate the hardships endured by generations of Laxey men. The statue was made in Bali by artist Ongky Wijana. Carved from a 5-tonne block of Carlow Blue limestone, it took him ten months to complete in his studio in Banjar Silakarang, Indonesia, before shipment to Laxey. Next we come to Brown's Café, the last of the refreshment establishments which were once so numerous among the houses on our left – Dumbell's Row – that they earned it the nickname 'Ham & Egg Terrace'. As we proceed along Mines Road we pass the gift shop of Laxey and Lonan Heritage Trust, a good place to pick up books, tickets or local information, which occupies the original village fire station. Further on we pass the current Laxey Fire Station, which in turn occupies the site of the former Mines Yard. Here would have been located the blacksmiths who produced much of the equipment used underground, as well as pay offices, gunpowder stores, stables for ponies and other administrative buildings.

Continue to the end of Mines Road and take a sharp ninety-degree right turn, followed by an equally sharp ninety-degree left turn. You are now in the Laxey Wheel carpark, and admission to the monument is via the kiosk at the top. As you enter the site, follow the path to the right. You will see the ruins of a cottage, once a traditional Manx thatched building consisting of a living and cooking area, bedroom and cockloft above. Known as the Cabin, it once housed a miner and his eight children. Continue along this path to the entrance to the Old Adit. Here you can experience a little of what life was like for the Laxey miners of the nineteenth century as they tunnelled their way through hard rock. Returning along the same path there are good views of the Wheel and the rod duct which transmitted the power to the pumps at the top of the Engine Shaft. Dumbell could have constructed the Wheel at the head of the shaft and obviated the need for the duct, but he chose instead to position it where it would have maximum visibility and impact in the village below.

Crossing the small bridge brings us to the bottom of the wheelcase. Steps take the more intrepid visitor to the very top of the Wheel, where magnificent views can be had over the village of Laxey and beyond. For those with sufficient time, a walk further up the valley along the Mines Trail reveals the cistern, a stone pit in which water was collected to drive the Wheel, as well as the ruins of the Engine House, Compressor House, and entrance to the Welsh Shaft. Be aware, however, that the paths are steep and often muddy following wet weather. Stout shoes are essential, and you should allow at least an hour.

Back in the car park it is now time to retrace our steps back along Mines Road to the carpark opposite Dumbell's Row. Leave the car here and cross over the main road for a chance to explore the landscaped Washing Floors, where lead and zinc ore was once crushed and sorted. Although the miners' statue commemorates a male figure, it should be borne in mind that the Washing Floors were operated almost exclusively by women and children, in conditions of extreme hardship. The smaller waterwheel here is the Lady Evelyn, once a working wheel at a shaft higher up the valley, until it was sold to a Cornish mine. It was returned to the Island and restored by mining enthusiasts in 2006. When trains are operating, visitors can also access the restored Great Laxey Mine railway at this point. The two miniature steam engines, Ant & Bee, are faithful replicas of those used by the mining company to haul ore from the mine to the Washing Floors. They make use of a restored and renovated section of original tunnel. This once carried the railway under the enormous pile of waste rock (the 'deads') which dominated this part of the village. In fact, at 75.8 yards in length, this is the longest railway tunnel on the Isle of Man. Returning to the car, rejoin the main road. Turn left, heading for Ramsey. As we leave Laxey a sign is visible on the left indicating the location of **King Orry's Grave**, along Ballaragh Road. The site is actually a Neolithic monument, constructed many centuries before King Orry arrived on the Island. If you chose to visit, keep an eye open for the house on the left with peculiar stones protruding from the gable end, situated just before you reach the monument. These are known in Manx as *Boid Sugganes*, and are the protruding stones to which a thatched roof was fixed. This house was clearly once thatched, and has had an additional storey added at some point in its history.

Return to the A2, and continue heading north until you reach the right turn marked A15 Maughold. Keep following the signs for Maughold until you reach the village, or if you wish, take a minor right-hand turn marked Ballaglass Glen. This will take you south towards **Cashtal yn Ard**. The Neolithic chambered tomb is on high ground and gives spectacular views, but be warned the road becomes quite narrow, and at times is single track with minimal passing places. There is also only room for about one car to park by the gate. Then there is a short walk of about ¼ mile to the site. Returning to the A15, St Maughold's church and churchyard are directly beyond the village green. The churchyard is within a locality which included medieval ecclesiastical lands, those held by St Bees, a religious house on the coast of north-western England, and those held by the Island's bishop, a medieval baron of the kingdom, who also held lands elsewhere on the Island. By the fourteenth century, the church of St Maughold's had been appropriated to Furness Abbey. The monastery apparently still held the church at the time of its dissolution, based on related entries in the accounts of the agents of the English crown.

William and Constance Radcliffe, local historians of both Maughold and Bride parishes, were among the first to note the unusual size of Kirk Maughold's churchyard. At more than 3½ acres, it is the largest of the traditional parish churchyards in the Isle of Man. It is also unusual in other ways. In addition to St Maughold's church, with incorporated medieval fabric, it contains the remains of three keeills, with the known site of a fourth. This configuration is significant and St Maughold's has been compared with a series of early ecclesiastical sites in Scotland: East Burra (Shetland), Applecross (Wester Ross), St Andrews (Fife), Whithorn, and Iona. These sites all share evidence of high status, be that royal, ecclesiastical, or both, and all had multiple churches or chapels within the perimeter. By contrast, the site is also unique in a Manx context. It is not a typical placement for the keeills, which characteristically occur as individual chapels, found in the arable farmland or more remote areas.

The possible interpretations for St Maughold's are assisted by a consideration of the carved and inscribed monuments associated with the churchyard. Addressing the early Manx stones, historian Ross Trench-Jellicoe has stated that this level of literacy and sophistication is unlikely to be encountered elsewhere other than at a monastic site. A later carved stone, the 'Saints' Slab', displays iconography linking it to similar monuments in eastern Scotland. The stone was recovered in the mid-nineteenth century from the church building itself, where it had been reused as part of an external stairway. The slab presents a ring-head cross, with a pair of facing saints. Dressed in hooded robes, the figures are positioned in the quadrants below the cross-head. Based on the linkage with Scotland, the saints may represent two Desert Fathers, Paul and Anthony, another indicator of monastic association. The probable date for this latter stone is some time in the ninth century.

These are far from the only stones preserved at St Maughold's. The open-air Cross House displays a wealth of these memorial monuments. In addition to the carved stones recovered from the churchyard itself, there are also stones that were brought in from the area of the traditional parish, a custom observed elsewhere in Mann. P. M. C. Kermode's *Manx Crosses* often records the places and circumstances of such recoveries, a matter of ongoing interest in the Isle of Man.

Return along the Maughold Road to rejoin the A2 heading into Ramsey. Follow the road until it divides, taking the right-hand fork named Stanley Mount; from here you can see Queen's Pier. Originally used for mooring large passenger ships in deeper water out in the bay, the pier had a miniature steam engine reputed to be the inspiration for the Reverend W.H. Audrey's *Thomas the Tank Engine*. Stanley Mount will lead you to Queen's Promenade and ultimately to South Promenade where you will find another interesting, if more recent, church dedicated to St Maughold, which serves the local Roman Catholic population.

In 1910, this new church was completed on land adjacent to the chapel of St Maughold. It is representative of the early work of a noted English architect, Sir Giles Gilbert Scott. The simplicity of the interior focuses attention on the intense colour of the area of the high altar. The church's location on the promenade, facing the sea, resulted in a 'liturgical east' in the western end of the church. A massive tower at the eastern end, instead of the more traditional 'west tower', completes the central structure. Scott's work also included an attached presbytery, a priest's house, to the north. The site of the former chapel became the garden of the presbytery, with the chapel's northern wall, the location of the previous high altar, preserved as a shrine. Thus, the nineteenth-century dedication to St Maughold was carried over into the newly established whole. With architectural significance and historic value, Our Lady, Star of the Sea, and Saint Maughold is also a registered building.

If you have parked the car in the Market Place car park, then you are well placed for 'Caroline Corner'. Within sight of you is the Commercial Hotel (now known as the Ellan Vannin pub), where DJs would stay on their way to and from the famous pirate radio ship. A little further along the harbour and you will come to number 9, East Street, which was Radio Caroline's Ramsey office. From here it's a twenty-minute walk or a short journey in the car, across the swing bridge over the harbour, and along Old River Road behind the swimming pool. When you reach North Shore Road turn right and continue to the end. From this point in 1968 you would have been able to see the MV *Caroline* on the horizon, framed in the gap in the sea wall between the two square pillars.

If you are interested in visiting Milntown House, you need to head back into the town and take the A3 Lezayre Road heading west for a short distance; the house is on the left-hand side of the road. The Christian Family lived at Milntown from at least the early sixteenth century and parts of the house date from that period; extensive alterations and additions were made during the seventeenth century. After this period the Christians moved to Cumberland and let the house out to tenants, but in 1830 Deemster John Christian returned to live in Milntown after having the mansion house substantially redesigned to the way it appears today. Following the death of William Bell Christian in 1886, the house was run first as a private school by his widow, Vio, and their two daughters, Rita and May, and then as a hotel.

It reverted to being a family home when Charles Peel Yates (of Yates' Wine Lodges) bought it in 1947.

The interior of the house is as decorated and furnished by Lady Edwards and her son Sir Clive prior to his death in 1999 but there are still many features dating from Deemster Christian's 1830 refurbishment and earlier periods. The front of the house includes the coats of arms of the Christian family and that of Sir Clive Edwards, and is in the Gothic Revival style. Milntown is usually open for house tours every Wednesday and Saturday at 2.30 pm from end of March to end of September (excluding MGP and TT race weeks). Admission costs £7 per person. Booking is recommended as places are limited. Private house tours for fifteen or more individuals can be booked upon request.

Following the A3 to the west for about another half mile will bring you to a footpath on the left-hand side of the road. This will lead you to a stone monument at the foot of Sky Hill, which commemorates the battle which was fought in this area in 1079, between the Manx and the forces of Godred Crovan. As no firm archaeological evidence for the battle has so far come to light however, the location must remain somewhat speculative.

A visit to Milntown is complimented by a tour of the other large house in the Ramsey area, the Gibb family home called the Grove. From Ramsey town centre take the A9 heading north towards Andreas. As we reach the outskirts of Ramsey on the left-hand side you will see Manx National Heritage signs for the Grove Museum. A tour of this Victorian mansion really deserves an hour, especially if the weather is favourable and there are flowers to admire in the gardens. A good indicator of the development of Ramsey comes from the fact that when the Gibb sisters (who were the last of their family to live at the Grove) were children, there was hardly another house north of the stone bridge over the Sulby River. Now, the Grove is surrounded by extensive housing estates, the products of the 1960s building boom. At the Grove you will find period rooms set out as they would have been in the era of the Gibbs, and knowledgeable site staff will be able to tell you more about the family. There is also a café and giftshop on site.

If your interest lies in aviation history, rejoin the A9 heading north towards Andreas and its airfield. As you approach, across the fields to your left you will see Andreas church. During the Second World War the steeple was reduced in height to avoid the risk of collision with aircraft, because the church aligns with one of the runways. It was intended to rebuild the spire after the war, but this never happened. Once in the village, take the right-hand fork on to Oatlands Road. Follow this around until it bends sharply to the left, and take the right-hand fork marked 'Private Road'. A number of the former airfield buildings such as the control tower are visible from this road. Some have now been converted to light industrial use and are private property. Andreas airfield has two runways, which are still used by gliding and flying clubs. Visitors must consider these to be active at all times and must check that no aircraft are moving, or on landing approach before entering any runway. Vehicles moving on the airfield must use hazard warning lights at all times. Headlights are recommended before moving on a runway.

Returning to Andreas village, pick up the A17 heading south, towards Kerroogarrow. This Civil-War-era fort now stands isolated in farmland, but once dominated an important route across the north of the Island. Situated at map reference SC 405 970, the site is indicated by a green sign. Leave the car on the main road, and be prepared for a fair walk across farm land. After visiting Kerroogarrow, head south once more along the A17 to pick up the A13 then A14 heading to Jurby. The first thing that the visitor notices when approaching Jurby from this direction is the fact that the road crosses a runway. Following the closure of the RAF station in 1963, the airfield was used as a diversion for Ronaldsway Airport. In order to be able to accept Vickers Viscount turboprop airliners the main East/West runway was extended eastwards and bisected by the Sandygate Road (A14). To facilitate the use of the extended runway, barriers were placed across the road and the road was closed while the runway was in use. Many original features of the site are readily identifiable, from bomb shelters, to control tower and store rooms. Another museum worth at least an hour is located here – the Manx Heritage Transport Trust Museum, located in an original RAF Bellman hangar. Designed by N.S. Bellman, the Royal Air Force Directorate of Works structural engineer, it is one of four transportable hangars built at Jurby during the winter of 1939/40, to the same design and one of around 400 built in total. The museum is constantly changing and at the time of writing exhibits include a 1950 Fordson E83W van, a 1950's Dennis Fire engine wheel escape and a 1938 Ford drop-head convertible.

Pick up the A10 skirting the airfield once more and head south to the junction with Ballavarran Road. Turn right along a minor road to visit Jurby church. A medieval record of 1291 held by The National Archives at Kew contains one of the earliest references to 'the church of St Patrick, Dureby, in Man'. It records that a chaplain had been assigned to Jurby by the English king, Edward I, because the Isle of Man was in his hands at that point. The present successor to that building stands at the end of Church Road. Sited on a rising headland near the sea, Jurby Church is a landmark on Mann's northern plain. The present church was raised in the early nineteenth century, with a distinctive bell tower which was of unusual height. A previous, smaller church had become ruinous by 1812, and its replacement was planned for a new location, on the south side of the existing churchyard. The older church was to be taken down, with the materials reused in the construction of a new church with a single-aisle nave. The completed structure would hold thirty-six pews, each able to seat eight persons, which illustrates the population of what, 200 years on, is now a rather sparsely inhabited part of the Island. Jurby church is bordered on the north side by the original churchyard and to the east by a newer extension to accommodate further burials. The older area incorporates a probable Viking burial mound, within the still discernible bank of an early cemetery. The cemetery's northern edge is curved; the walled western boundary has a level noticeably higher than the land outside the wall. The eastern extension of the churchyard has more modern graves, including those of a series of casualties related to the Royal Air Force presence at Jurby in the Second World War. These were pilots and crew members killed in training accidents, and include airmen from the United Kingdom, Canada, Poland, The Netherlands, and Australia, whose final resting place is marked by the Commonwealth War Graves Commission. The twentieth-century war memorial, a ring-head cross, occupies the site of the previous church, to the immediate east of the older area of burials. The porch interior houses a series of Viking-age carved monuments, which would have been brought to the churchyard from within the area of the traditional parish. More than one integrates Christian iconography and artistic motifs associated with Norse storytelling. One particular figure has been interpreted as Heimdall, blowing the horn that will call the Norse gods and heroes to the last great battle of Ragnarök.

There are still unanswered questions regarding the relationship between the earlier church at Jurby, and a chapel to be found at West Nappin to the southwest. The remains of this structure stand in a large field, with a well-preserved eastern portion that indicates a late-medieval church. Though this is under the care of Manx National Heritage, it should be noted that the ruins now stand on private land. It is also unclear as to whom this chapel was dedicated. Around 1900, Father Gillow of Ramsey wrote a history of the Catholic faith in the Ramsey area, and noted:

> At the Nappin, Jurby, we find in the middle of a large field, the remains of what was once a Catholic Church. The northeast gable has a three-light window, embedded in the orthodox red sandstone. In the southeast wall, in the corner, are the two niches for the wine and water cruets, and underneath, the Sacrarium. I was informed that some 200 years ago, the building was cut through the middle in order to make a school. This church was dedicated to St. Patrick, and the east and southeast gables, which are still standing, afford ample evidence of its former uses as a Catholic place of worship.[27]

However another source tells us of a different dedication:

> This tiny keeill, Church of St Cecilia, has a remarkable history. Originally a Bronze Age tumulus, it became a Christian 'cell' probably falling into decay in the Middle Ages until in 1749 Thomas Clarke, of The Nappin, restored and enlarged it to make a day school for the children of the neighbourhood. Now it stands, a bleak little ruin, probably unique.
>
> Where else would one find in so tiny a building traces of an early Christian Piscina, a window of the Middle Ages and an eighteenth century schoolroom fireplace?[28]

From here follow the A10 coast road south, following the sign for Ballaugh when you reach The Cronk. This will bring you back to the A3 TT course. Turn right here, and follow the A3. Just after you pass the Bishopscourt National Glen, you will see a large house on the right. Now a private residence, this was once the seat of the bishops of Sodor and Mann. The square tower, which comprises the oldest part of the house, and which is probably medieval in date, is clearly visible from the pavement. Bishopscourt Glen is publicly accessible, and covers about 5 hectares stretching from the high road for around half a mile towards the hills. It is planted with mixed hardwoods and shrubs. The glen was formerly part of the private garden belonging to the bishops who resided at the house opposite the entrance. Many features such as the small lakes created from mill ponds were developed by previous bishops and their families, in particular by Lady Murray, wife of Bishop Murray (circa 1815). At the entrance is an artificial hillock named Mount Aeolus. This was created by Bishop Hildesley to commemorate Captain Elliott's victory over a French squadron off the Manx coast on 28 February 1760. This battle saw the capture of three enemy vessels, under the command of Francois Thurot, and it was said that Hildesley watched the action from the shore. Afterwards, he set up the mast of one of the French ships on the mount, though it has since been lost to the elements.

Another feature is a small cave with a carved stone seat. This cave is thought to have been used by bishops for the purpose of rest and meditation. Bishop Murray reputedly took refuge here from angry locals at the time of the 1825 potato tithe riots. Nearby is a stone called Creg ny Ushag (Rock of the Bird) which is inscribed: 'Lead me to the rock that is higher than I', probably dating from about 1880.

From Bishopscourt follow the A3 back to Ballacraine where it joins the A1 Peel Road, and from here return to Douglas.

TOUR ROUTE 3

Peel and the West by Car

This tour takes in the western conurbation of Peel, as well as a number of other interesting sites en route and in the surrounding countryside. Head west out of Douglas along the Peel Road. Having negotiated Quarterbridge and passing the Jubilee Oak, we come to Old Kirk Braddan, and next to it its newer counterpart. Old Kirk Braddan was at one time the main burial ground for the expanding town of Douglas, and the jumbled mass of graves in the churchyard reflect the pressure that it was under. One tomb in particular is of interest – the obelisk of Arran granite stone, bearing the three legs of Mann, marks the final resting place of Lord Henry Murray, brother of the Duke of Atholl, commander of the Royal Manx Fencibles, and Lieutenant Governor of the Isle of Man until his death aged just 38. This was brought about by his dissolute lifestyle, and one obituary stated that Lord Henry was 'a martyr to dissipation'. At the other end of the social spectrum, Old Kirk Braddan churchyard also contains the headstone of Samuel Ally, a man born a slave, but given his freedom by Manxman Sir Mark Wilks. It reads:

> An African and native of St Helena. Died the 28th of May 1822 aged 18 years. Born a slave, and exposed to the corrupt influences of that unhappy state, he became a model of TRUTH and PROBITY for the more fortunate of any country or condition.
>
> This stone is erected by a grateful master to the memory of a faithful servant who repaid the boon of Liberty with unbounded attachment.

Continuing along Peel Road we soon reach the village of Union Mills. Keep a look out for the Post Office on the right hand side of the road, with its blue plaque marking its association with the Bee Gees pop group. Passing through Crosby, and just before we reach the Highlander Inn we pass the ruins of St Trinian's church. It should be noted that the building is situated on private land though a good view can be had from the public highway.

Further on, we pass Greeba Castle and Greeba Towers (both private residences) visible on the right high above the road and through the trees. It is said that the builder of Greeba Castle (a wealthy Liverpool ship owner) was an inveterate gambler who lost the house on the turn of a card. He honoured his bet, but claimed the wager did not cover the grounds, and so built himself an almost identical property (Greeba Towers) on the land that he retained.

Passing through the traffic lights at Ballacraine we come to St Johns. This is the location of the annual Tynwald Day ceremony each midsummers day, a tradition dating back to Viking times. Tynwald Hill itself is said to be composed of sods of earth from every parish on the Island. Down a minor road, leading away from the hill towards Ballig to the north, you will find the Giant's Grave, a Bronze Age tomb from around 1000 BC. The burial cist was once covered by a circular mound, but has now been exposed on one side, by the cutting for the road. The rest of the monument remains covered by a raised earth bank which was partially restored in 1954. To the south of the main road are the Ballahara stones. These come from a neolithic tomb, dating from around 2300 BC. However they are not in situ, having been found during excavations at a local sand quarry, and later re-erected at St Johns. The Tynwald Visitor Centre is located at Fairfield House on the Main Road. In the centre, visitors can find out about 'thing sites' like Tynwald around the world, look at old photos of St John's, learn about calendar customs, see how Tynwald works, and marvel at a Lego model of Tynwald Day. Younger visitors can choose from colouring-in, dressing up and playing with some Lego to add to the model. Tynwald Hill itself is accessible to visitors through out the year except for Tynwald Day itself, when it becomes the centre of formal proceedings.

Continuing along the A1, we come to Peel, the Island's western metropolis and often considered to be the most Manx in character of its towns and villages. Unlike Douglas, Ramsey and Castletown, Peel retains much of its quaint charm as a fishing port, with winding lanes and picturesque cottages. Strictly speaking Peel is a city, as it is home to St German's Cathedral, and is the seat of the Bishop of Sodor and Mann. A good place to start your visit is the **House of Manannan**. The heritage centre explores the Viking and maritime history of the Isle of Man, introduces the visitor to some famous Manx seafaring characters, and provides the background to Peel Castle and St Patrick's Isle. As you explore you are guided by the reassuring words of Manannan himself, who appears on video screens in a variety of guises. You should allow two hours to see the House of Manannan properly, and more if you have purchased a combined ticket to explore Peel Castle as well.

Adjacent to the town of Peel, St Patrick's Isle dominates the view from both the town's waterfront and Peel Hill. Administered by Manx National Heritage, the islet is a major focus for tourism, with access via a pedestrian causeway. It has also been the subject of extended archaeological work. Excavations carried on between 1982 and 1988 substantially modified older assumptions about the site. One of the archaeologists involved, Ross Trench-Jellicoe, believes that it led to a fundamental reorientation of the historical picture. Previously, St Patrick's Isle has been likened to the parish churchyard at Maughold as the potential site of an early Christian monastery. However, none of the excavations so far have produced any convincing evidence to substantiate such a claim. While the extensive graveyards in the explored areas of St Patrick's Isle are firm witnesses to the long-standing presence of Christianity on the site, none of the indicators which might prove the presence of an early monastery has been recovered here.

A more detailed interpretation of the carved monuments recovered on the isle provides further insights. With few exceptions, the stones display a 'rustic' design and craftsmanship suggesting that they originated in lay, or secular, cemeteries. The external area of cultural influence appears to be the hinterland of Dublin, with northern Wales and the western isles of Scotland as other possibilities. In addition to providing a geographic orientation, the analysis of the stones supports an association with secular rather than monastic communities. Interestingly, this Christian cemetery was the site of one of the most spectacular pagan Viking graves to have been found in the British Isles. A woman had been buried with the rich trappings appropriate to her status in life, in preparation for an equally impressive existence in the afterlife, which the Vikings believed followed their earthly existence. The Pagan Lady, as she has come to be known, can be seen in the House of Manannan, and her possessions are on display at the Manx Museum. They

The ruins of St German's Cathedral within Peel Castle

include an iron rod, a possible symbol of domestic authority, an unique necklace of over seventy glass, amber and jet beads, knives, a comb, shears for cutting cloth, and needles. Six other pagan graves, none of them quite as impressive as hers, were also found nearby, but of equal significance is that they form a tiny part of a much larger Christian cemetery.

The Chronicles of Mann serve as an interpretive framework for the finds that could be dated to the period of the dynasty of Godred Crovan. The discoveries support the idea of the isle as a probable royal fortification, with evidence for domestic habitation. The latter was confirmed through the recovery of evidence for a high-status Norse structure, datable to the twelfth century. The existing cathedral ruins within Peel Castle may relate to the new church mentioned in the Chronicles, begun in or before 1248. At the very least, it is probable that the remains of this smaller church lie at the core of the surviving structure.

According to the Chronicles, the new church carried a dedication to Germanus, but it may not have been the first on the islet with that dedication. The exact identity of this saint is uncertain, with some sources claiming Germanus as the successor of St Patrick. In the *Book of Armagh*, however, Germanus of Auxerre is the Continental saint who sends Patrick to Ireland. Germanus plays a similar enabling role in the *Historia Brittonum*, originally a work of the ninth century. In various forms, it circulated in Wales, England, and Ireland, as well as on the Continent.

The ruins of St Patrick's church, dated to the eleventh century, stand on the highest point of St Patrick's Isle. St Patrick's church has an east window, but the doorway is located at the western end of the north wall. The walls are constructed of local stone, including red sandstone. The structure exhibits evidence for multiple phases of modification, and indeed for a local population of significant size. For example, the existing ruins present an interior size more than three times that of the medieval chapel at Jurby. With interior measurements in an approximate 3:1 ratio, the surviving structure also appears to share the relative dimensions noted by P. M. C. Kermode for the early parish churches in the Isle of Man.

There is a contemporary detached round tower to the west, which aligns with the church. The tower is typically Irish in style, and is one of only three outside of Ireland; the remaining two are in eastern Scotland. Sometimes known as bell-houses, these are usually constructed in relationship to a specific church. Curiously, the complex and innovative architecture of these bell-houses tends to be paired with conservative church structures of significantly less sophistication. It has also been noted that the round towers tend to occur at sites also associated with secular kingship.

St Patrick's chapel is located near the centre of the islet, to the northeast of St Patrick's church. The relationship between the two structures is not fully understood; Kermode compared structure of the chapel to that of the earlier keeills, but considered it to be a more advanced form. The walls are of local stone, including red and yellow sandstone; the chapel has an east window and the usual western doorway. It may be that this was a private chapel, while St Patrick's church served the local parishioners.

Indeed it appears that St Patrick's church on the islet continued to be the Kirk Patrick parish church well into the post-medieval period. However, at some point probably around 1550, the Patrick parishioners began worshipping at an alternate location, St Peter's church in Peel itself, where they had their own aisle. According to local tradition, the decision to move was made when the people of Patrick parish lost a coffin to the sea on the way to St Patrick's Isle for a funeral. In 1872 a clock was presented to St Peters by the Honourable J.K. Ward of Montreal and as there was no place to put it, a new tower was built to house it. It ceased to be parish church when what is now Peel Cathedral was opened in 1893, and afterwards had a number of uses. A fire in 1958 virtually destroyed it, and most of the remains apart from the clock tower were removed. Today the site of St Peter's is preserved in the lozenge-shaped area of Peel's old marketplace.

In the seventeenth century James Stanley improved the defences of the castle against possible attack. He added two loop-holed walls within the castle walls for musketeers. This created a 'killing ground' in which enemy infantry who succeeded in gaining entry to the castle would be cut down. Adjacent to the ruins of the apartments of the earls of Derby, sheltered from the prevailing wind by the rising ground behind them, are the remains of the Napoleonic battery built in the early nineteenth century. The view from here clearly shows the field of fire commanded by this battery, which was built to defend Peel Bay from attack from the sea. An audio guide is available at the castle, providing much more detail on the various features within.

The **Leece Museum** situated in the Old Courthouse on East Quay is devoted to objects, photographs and documents specifically relating to Peel. Before leaving, don't forget to visit the Black Hole prison cell underneath the court house, where wrongdoers were incarcerated in days gone by. There are still some reminders in the cell of the days when a prison term was imposed for the simplest of offence, such as chains on the walls. If your time permits, why not also book a tour of **Moore's Kipper Yard**, on Mill Road behind the House of Manannan. Kipper smoking was once a major Manx industry and kippers were a famous Manx export. Moore's is a family run business and a working factory with an on-site shop selling traditionally oak-smoked products as well as local seafoods. You can even arrange to have kippers delivered by post to friends and family. The tours normally run for thirty minutes, depending on the size of the group, and take visitors through the entire kipper-making process. There is a charge of £2 per person (see the company website for more details).

Leaving Peel, head south on the A27. Shortly after crossing the river Neb we come upon the site of the First World War internment camp at Knockaloe, latterly the Isle of Man government's experimental farm. Only a few buildings remain from the camp, including the meat storehouse and an engine shed built as part of the specially constructed railway line from St Johns. Some years back a plaque was placed on the engine shed by the Anglo-German Family History Society, to mark the enormous part that this camp played in the lives of many Germans who had settled in Britain. Opposite the entrance is St Patrick's church, and in the churchyard behind may still be found some of the graves of those internees who died here between 1914 and 1918.

Previously the residents of Patrick parish had been forced to travel to St Peters in Peel to attend church, but in 1710, the Island's bishop noted the difficult situation of the people of this parish, without a church of their own. He laid out plans for the provision of a new parish church, and committed to the process of freeing the Patrick parishioners from financial obligations to St Peter's. Early in the eighteenth century, the Radcliffe family had offered land from the Knockaloe estate for a new parish church and churchyard. The site already had religious associations for it reportedly contained an ancient keeill. In 1760, a report of the Highways Committee referred to it as 'Kirkpatrick Church'. By 1879, the building was considered to be beyond repair, and the churchyard required expansion for additional burials. The plan at that time was to build a small mortuary chapel at the Knockaloe site, with the land previously occupied by the church added to the churchyard for burials. A larger parish church was to be built later on, at a new site in Glen Maye, some distance away. It was never built, and the mortuary chapel eventually became the official parish church for Kirk Patrick Parish. The adjacent schoolroom now houses a recently opened visitor centre, exploring life in Knockaloe Camp.

The churchyard also has military burials from the First World War, guards from the camp, or men who died of wounds or else while at home on leave. An interesting contemporary account, published just after the war, comments:

> Sentimentalising over the country's enemies, you say? One would not spare a sigh for any of them if by so doing one cheated a British soldier of a sigh, and one is quite prepared to question whether the friends of an Englishman who had died in a German camp would have been permitted to place over his remains that quotation about the Lord giving him rest from his enemies. And yet — the man who hit upon that text may have lived in England all his life, may have never had the smallest desire to do England harm, and may have been taken from his home and business and dragged to the other end of the country at a minute's notice. If one were wandering through any other churchyard, one would not read without emotion such inscriptions as 'Here rests, far from his home, Robert Peltzer ... Erected by his friends and compatriots,' or this legend at the bottom of another memorial, 'He was a good comrade.' One or two of the inscriptions are actually in English throughout, and there is a stone which covers the remains of William Brown and William Howard. And it does not seem altogether a sacrilege that directly adjacent to these tombstones should be thirteen stone crosses erected 'To the Glory of God, and to the memory of the following soldier who died in the service of King and Country —' with the name of some member of the Royal Defence Corps who died while guarding the same camp in which these aliens were interned. One of these crosses denotes the grave of Pte. Michael Carroll, who was drowned in the torpedoing of the passenger steamer 'Leinster', and elsewhere in the

churchyard are interred the bodies of two unknown women, washed up on the Patrick coast, who were lost from the same vessel. A similar tragedy of the sea is commemorated by a cross bearing the inscription, 'British – Unidentified. Date of Burial, 27/2/18.' And in the days to come, when the natural passions aroused by the great world conflict have subsided, our descendants will probably look at the graves of the German prisoners and of the British soldiers, and reflect that they were all alike sharers, and to a great extent involuntary sharers, in sorrow.[29]

Continue to follow the A27 south through the village of Glen Maye (where it does a sharp dogleg) until you reach the minor right-hand turn signposted for Niarbyl (a useful landmark in the form of a red telephone kiosk stands on the left-hand side of the road here). Proceed down to the Niarbyl cafe on the left-hand side at the bottom of the Niarbyl Road. As you do so, keep an eye open for wartime buildings in the fields on the right. This was once the site of RAF Dalby, a Chain Home radar station during the Second World War. The Niarbyl Cafe was originally an ex-Knockaloe Camp hut, repurposed in the 1920s as a tourist venue, to serve the many visitors who came this way by means of war-surplus charabancs. Leave the car in the carpark and take a short walk down to the shoreline. Here you will find charming eighteenth-century thatched cottages, as well as the holiday home of Edwardian musical hall star Florrie Ford. The Niarbyl area is steeped in folklore and local legend. The most famous of these is the story of the

The picturesque thatched cottages at Niarbyl. They have featured in numerous productions including 1998's Waking Ned

Water Kilpie, whose sweet music enchanted the people of the area. Folklorist Sophia Morrison made a note of the tune, and wrote:

> In the long ago a curiously shaped boat would be seen at the close of a summer evening coming from Bradda towards Dalby. In the boat sat an old man with long white hair, who rowed until off Niarbyl Point; there he rested on his oars and sang this melody, which runs up and down the minor scale with the lilt of the waves. And as the thing became known, the people would come and stay on the shore to listen to his music, for it was very sweet to them; but his boat was far off, and no words could be distinguished. When the old man had made an end of the song, he rowed south-westward till he was seen no more. And no one knew whence he came, nor whither he went, nor who he was, but the people of Dalby knew his song and taught it to their children's children.[30]

Niarbyl, sheltered as it is from the North East wind, was in fact a major fishing base at one point, with more than thirty vessels operating from here. The channel, which was known as the Barra (meaning passage or inlet), is still discernible, cut through the rock from low water to half flood. Some of the boulders were also piled up to make a sort of quay. Many of the fishermen who came here were from Ireland, they came over in open boats called Swassals, fishing for lobsters. At night these men would pull their boats into the caves, and use them to sleep in. Some say it was these Irish fishermen who created the Barra. There was also some fishing for oysters here, but it was not a great success. Another source tells us:

> The fishing was much more localised here than in Peel or Port St Mary, because the Dalby boats were owned by farmers and crofters who only went to the fishing between the seasons of intensive farm work, and did not join in the long voyages to Lerwick or the seasons at Kinsale. These boats were smaller, and were known as Scoutts.

> They were open boats, usually depending on oars but also stepping a lug sail, and they worked mostly around the Manx coasts, with occasional trips to Northern Ireland. This was two way traffic, for Irish boats used to come over in the summer for the lobster fishing, and berth at Niarbyl for the whole season.

Peel fishermen sometimes joined those of Dalby, for in some winds it was difficult to land at Peel before the breakwater was built, so the boats used to make round to Niarbyl which was sheltered.[31]

When they landed the catch here, an impromptu fish market was held on the beach, with fish dealers bidding and carts waiting to load up. Cod was the main catch in winter, and most of the Dalby folk dried a store of it, besides salting-down herring. Niarbyl seems to have been eclipsed by Peel about 1875 and most of the boats moved there, probably as a result of the breakwater being built in Peel, but also one source tells us, it was because of the effort involved in hauling boats out of the water here.

At one time five families lived around the bay – three in the two surviving cottages and what is now a ruin of one adjacent, one in a cottage now covered by Florrie Forde's hut, and one in a sod cottage by the footpath leading down to the shore, which can just still be made out at the right time of the year. At this time, three of the five houses on this beach sold beer, and there were said to be twenty such pubs between Dalby and Glen Maye, as no licence was then required. It is reported that the beer was mostly Castletown Ale, the barrels of which were brought overland by horse-drawn sledge.

One of the families were the Cashens – William Cashen was a Manx speaker and folklorist, later custodian of Peel castle; he was born in 1838 in Dalby, but moved to these cottages when he was a boy. Like many Manxmen, his father was a part-time fisherman and part-time farmer. William Cashen was brought up in the endmost of the cottages, with nine brothers and sisters. He would say that he and his brothers slept in the cock loft with their noses nearly touching the scraa, that not a window in the cottage opened, and not a doctor ever darkened the door! The Niarbyl beach was his playground as soon as he could walk, and here he remembered the 'childher' ran about while his mother worked in the house. He remembered his mother singing sweetly as she rocked the baby to sleep. When he was older he would go to see a weaver woman in Dalby and filled the bobbins for her, while she recited poetry to him in Manx.

Another account, however, tells how bad it could be here in a south-westerly gale, when the tide would actually come into the houses, and on one particular occasion the family had to put the child's crib on the table. Another family living in these cottages was that of Nan Watterson. She started a folk museum in one, and was serving teas in the cottage in the 1890s. This was one of the earliest museums on the Isle of Man. Her daughter Annie Clague was also a Manx speaker and contributed to the Manx Museum's folk life survey. She recalled:

> I was 3½ years old when I went to the beach to live. People used to do all their own baking at home, barley, oat and flour bread. Each person did not have a plate. People used to drink out of basins. There would often be a big milk dish of pinjane [curds and whey] and a spoon at them taking pinjane on to their plates. When killing pigs most people would share out or sell it to to their neighbours. Brawn would be made of the heart and scraps. We were making pancakes galore, too. Some ones would buy beer when the milk was scarce, putting it on the porridge instead of milk. There was a three legged craw and the kettle was put on this with ling under it to hurry it. There was an old man living downside of us, in a house with an earth floor white-washed round the edge, and a whole shovel full of sand put in the middle of the floor. There was an iron pot with handles to lift it away when not required. This type of portable grate would take the herring roaster in front or on top of it. My grandmother could spin according to what was required and then it would be sent to dyers for colour. I remember my mother having a blue frock made from thread spun on this wheel and woven by Jack Cain, the weaver who had his loom on the Niarbyl in the old cottage by the café.[32]

If you have time to explore further, Lag ny Keeilley (meaning 'Hollow of the Chapel') is a remote keeill sitting at the foot of Cronk ny Irree Laa ('Hill of the Rising Day'). It is accessed by public footpath past the house at Eary Cushlin, which is itself reached from the A27 Dalby Road. The footpath is over a mile long and is very narrow in places, and there is a steep drop down to the sea; it is therefore not advisable to take small children or anyone unsteady on their feet. In the 1920s the *Isle of Man Examiner* reported that:

> ... perhaps the best byway of all is the coast way to Lag-ny-Keeilley in the west. You must follow the road south from Glen Meay and Dalby, both attractive

places, but not to be lingered in if you desire even better things. Down into the great Dalby Lag dips our track, and then climbs steeply along the high savage cliffs to a deserted farm on the seaward side of Cronk-ny-Irree-Lhaa. Thence we follow a narrow path for almost two miles along the bare seaward face of the mountain, which drops almost sheer to the sea from the height of some 1,500 feet. At last the track descends, ending in a tiny green plateau some 300 feet above sea level, where are the remains of an ancient keeil chapel and hermit's cell. Here, centuries ago, lived a holy anchorite, and to his tiny church came there folk from far Dalby and scattered communities along the wild cliffs. A pleasant place it is wherein to spend a summer's afternoon, with the blue, clear water sounding below and the faint forms of the Irish mountains lifting across the channel, and the tall Cronk brooding above; a place worthy of pilgrimage and full of deep peace.[33]

Legend has it that this is the traditional burial-place of King Orry, or of the entire Orry line of the Norse kings, though there are other contenders for this title. When in the nineteenth century a brig was wrecked on the Calf, some of the bodies, which had drifted northward, were buried here; a place was levelled outside the keeill, and they were 'put under without any stones at them'. In the tradition of the community, there was a time when local Catholics were not allowed to use the churchyard of St Peter's for their burials. As a result, the burials took place on St Patrick's Isle or here at the mountainside keeill overlooking the sea, Lag ny Keeilley. The keeill is located in the southernmost part of the traditional parish of Kirk Patrick. The site remains important to the Catholic community in Mann even today. For perhaps a decade, Mass has been celebrated there on Tynwald Day, a time to pray for the Manx nation. There is yet another factor in the community's ties to Lag ny Keeilley. In the era when Catholic worship was forbidden, remote keeill sites on Mann's west coast are believed to have been used as meeting sites for local Catholics and Irish priests, who made clandestine visits to the Island by boat.

However, Catholic tradition does not associate the dedication of Lag ny Keeilley with St Patrick. It is linked to Dónart, a disciple of the Apostle of the Irish. From the altar area of the old chapel, the remains of the entrance align with a mountain peak across the Irish Sea, Sliabh Dónairt. It is the highest peak of the Mountains of Mourne, and both the saint and the mountain have a significant place in Irish tradition.

Returning to the Dalby Road, continue until you meet the A36 heading to Foxdale via the A3, which involves a left turn at the junction. As you make the turn, the view in front of you is dominated by the towering mass of South Barrule, the summit of which is crowned by an Iron Age hill fort. This again was once an area dominated by mining, and there are still ruins from that industry to be seen above ground. In particular, on your left you will see the, once much more impressive, chimney of Beckwith's Mine. This chimney had a distinct lean for many years but around half its height was lost in a collapse during a storm in 2012. The mine was first worked around 1839, and produced lead ore before being closed in 1877. The main shaft was 1,100ft deep, meaning that the bottom of it was considerably below sea level. Once in Foxdale turn right on the the A24 heading towards Douglas. This road in due course will take you past the Braaid, situated about halfway between Douglas and Foxdale, and one of the Island's most visually impressive archaeological sites. It contains an Iron Age roundhouse and two Viking-age longhouses, apparently occupied concurrently. The roundhouse was about 16.5 metres in diameter. Its structure was supported by massive standing stones around the circumference. The walls were then infilled with earth. The roof was made of turf placed on rafters made of brush and further supported by timber posts.

The two longhouses had differing purposes. The first was the main dwelling and had curved walls (resembling an upturned boat with ends cut off) made of turf with the gable ends made of timber. The roof was supported by two rows of posts standing on large stones. Like most Viking houses of the time, there were no internal walls. The house measured about 20 x 9 metres, which was large for its time and more than twice the norm. The second longhouse was used for cattle or other animals. This supposition was based upon the many stone stalls along the north wall. The roof was low and lightweight, and did not have the curved walls like the other longhouse. This building measured 18×8 metres.

Viking life centred around the home, which may account for the size of the main building, though the size of the constructs may indicate that the site was more than just a farmstead. The site occupies a fertile valley and would have been prime agricultural land in its time. It is tempting to speculate that it represents the intermarriage of an incoming Norse warrior with the Celtic nobility of the ninth century.

From here, follow the A24 eastwards until it becomes the A6 on the outskirts of Douglas. Turn left once you reach the roundabout on New Castletown Road (A5).

TOUR ROUTE 4

Castletown and the South by Car

This tour takes in the historic ancient capital of Mann, as well as some of the more interesting historic places to be discovered in the south of the Island. Start your tour by taking the old Castletown Road, which begins on the southern side of Douglas harbour. After about half a mile on the right you will pass the imposing stonework of the Nunnery gatehouse. As its name suggests this fine building (arguably once the finest private house on the Island after Castle Mona) stands on land once occupied by a religious order, disbanded during the Reformation. Nothing, save perhaps a few courses of stonework, now survives from the original building. Nor does the eighteenth-century house which once stood here still exist, for it was later replaced by a mansion in the Victorian Gothic style. It was occupied by the Heywood family in the eighteenth century before it passed to the Taubmans. For much of the twentieth century it was occupied by Colonel John Goldie-Taubmann, before being damaged in a fire. Later it was owned by the businessman and racehorse-owner Robert Sangster, who moved to the Isle of Man in 1975. Today it is occupied by a business school, part of University College Isle of Man.

Continue until you reach the large roundabout giving on to the A5 New Castletown Road, and turn left. The road will take you through Santon and over the Fairy Bridge – don't forget to say hello to the fairies, but do it in Manx so that they are sure to understand you – *Moghrey mie mooinjey veggey*! In fact this version of the Fairy Bridge is relatively recent. The original was nearer to Douglas, but was inaccessible to motor vehicles. When charabanc drivers began bringing tourists this way in the 1920s and 30s they transplanted the folkloric associations to a new bridge. Follow the road south until you reach Ballasalla. Here you may chose to turn right at the mini roundabout for **Rushen Abbey** (allow at least an hour for this visit, more if the weather is good and you wish to enjoy the grounds), or left for

Castletown. The left-hand turn takes you over the level crossing (also a good vantage point for photographing steam engines) and past Ronaldsway airport on your left. There are memorials to the Second World War units based here inside the terminal, but few of the surviving wartime buildings are visible if you are not actually airside (indeed take-off and landing on a clear day provide some of the best views of the bomb stores, fuel farm and pillboxes which still survive here). A much more evocative visit can be had at the adjacent **Manx Military and Aviation Museum**, housed partly in the old wartime photographic interpretation building. A good selection of bomb trolleys, propellers and other relics can be seen outside, while inside uniforms, maps and other memorabilia tell the story of the Island at war. The museum also holds the collection of the Manx Regiment (15th Light Anti Aircraft Regiment Royal Artillery), making for an absorbing visit. Again, you should allow at least an hour in order to do it justice.

Continue towards Castletown, passing the estate on your left known as Janet's Corner. The houses are built on the site of the camp which accommodated the personnel of HMS *Urley* (Ronaldsway), but today the only surviving wartime building is the camp cinema. As you reach the roundabout on the edge of Castletown, turn left along Shore Road and then left again onto the Promenade, leading to Derbyhaven Road. On your left is King William's College, a fee-paying school founded in the 1830s. It was once popular with army families, and some notable Victorian military figures were educated there, including Sir George White VC, who held the besieged town of Ladysmith during the Boer War. On your right is Hango Hill, once the location of a summer house used by the earls of Derby, and the execution site of Illiam Dhone. Turn right on to Fort Island Road and continue past the Golf Links Hotel until you reach Fort Island. This peninsula is important because it covers the entrance to Derbyhaven. The bay has always been the main route in and out of Castletown by sea, particularly as far as shipment of goods was concerned, as Castletown's own harbour was considered too dangerous.

There is evidence for human activity on the island from the Mesolithic period onward. It was also the site of two great battles for the control of the Isle of Man, firstly in 1250 and then again in 1275, when England, Scotland and the Manx were fighting for control of the Isle of Man. The Manx won the first battle, but twenty-five years later they lost control to Scotland. Two ancient buildings stand here. Both are in a state of ruin and closed to the public, though there are a number of walks which allow visitors to explore the surrounding countryside. St Michael's chapel, dating from the twelfth century, is on the south side of the island. This Celtic-Norse structure was built on the site of an older Celtic keeill. Derby Fort, a seventeenth-century gun battery, is at the eastern end of the island. It was built during the reign of Henry VIII, and re-armed in 1645 during the English Civil War by James Stanley, the 7th Earl of Derby and Lord of Mann, to protect the then busy port of Derbyhaven.

From here we retrace our steps and move on to Castletown itself, which has a wealth of attractions (enough indeed to justify a day in its own right). Perhaps it is best to start with **Castle Rushen**, which could easily fill two to three hours. Before you go inside, have a look at the famous single-handed clock, reputedly the gift to the Island of Elizabeth I, and the old police station designed by Baillie Scott, standing opposite the castle. The building was completed in 1901, and in 2018 came into the ownership of Manx National Heritage. Plans are under way to allow public access, though at the time of writing it is not yet clear what form this will take.

Cross the road to enter the castle via the heavily defended barbican. Within the imposing walls stands the keep, with its recently renovated drawbridge. Inside, period rooms are set out reflecting life at the castle during different eras of Stanley rule. Other rooms examine the role of the castle as the Island's prison. At the very top, the wall-walks give impressive views over Castletown, while at the bottom a dungeon can be found. After visiting the castle, perhaps the most logical place to go next is the Old Grammar School, for the two are intimately connected. The school was originally the chapel of St Mary and there is strong evidence to suggest that it was begun at the same time as the castle, under the rule of the Norse kings. It can be found about a minute's walk from the castle, on the town's main carpark. The two other major heritage sites in Castletown are also closely linked. To get to the **Nautical Museum** – again just a minute's walk from the castle – you will need to cross over the Cain Bridge near the mouth of the harbour. This bridge commemorates Major Robert Henry Cain VC, a Castletown resident who, during the Second World War, became the only Manxman ever to be awarded a Victoria Cross.

The Nautical Museum was once the boathouse of Captain George Quayle, of Bridge House, which you will also see as you pass over Cain Bridge. Innovator, eccentric, army officer and member of the House of Keys, Quayle was many things and discoveries are still being made in relation to his historic yacht the *Peggy*. The Nautical Museum has been the site of a major archaeological investigation in recent years, and conservation work on the *Peggy* is ongoing, ahead of a planned redevelopment a few years hence. Quayle once held a seat in the **Old House of Keys**, directly opposite the castle. Public sittings in the renovated building are held hourly at peak season, but you will find more information on timings and ticketing at the castle. After passing out of use as a legislative chamber the building had been variously a bank and a public library, but was in a poor state internally when it was acquired by Manx National Heritage. Painstaking research in archives revealed the type of carpet with which the building had once been

Balcony House, the home of Captain John Quilliam of Trafalgar fame

fitted, while careful study of original scraps still on the wall informed the choice of wallpaper and interior decoration scheme.

As you leave Castletown Square via Queen Street, you will pass Balcony House on the right. This was the home of Captain John Quilliam who served as first lieutenant of HMS *Victory* at Trafalgar and was a protege of Lord Nelson. Next, turn right onto Farrants Way, before joining Arbory Road. Just beyond Castle Rushen High School on your left you will see a windmill, now devoid of sails. You are now passing the former Witches Mill, once Gerald Gardner's Museum of Witchcraft, though now a private residence.

After leaving Castletown, continue to head south towards Port Erin, following the A5. After about a mile-and-a-half you will see a minor road to the left signed 'Pooilvash Quarry'. Travel along this road for about another half mile before leaving the car and taking the footpath to the site of Balladoole Viking ship burial. In fact, this impressive Ancient Monument comprises a Bronze Age tomb, a Norse boat burial, and an early Christian religious site all set on a hill with fantastic views over the Bay ny Carrickey looking towards Port St Mary.

After rejoining the A5 continue to head south to Port Erin. Take the right-hand turn (Castletown Road) and follow this towards the town centre. On the left is the **Port Erin Railway Museum**, located quite literally at the end of the line – on the platform of the most southerly stop on the Isle of Man Steam Railway. The museum charts the history of the steam-powered railway from its inception in 1873 to the present day, including the now defunct lines which used to serve Peel, Ramsey and Foxdale. Inside you will find steam engines and carriages including the royal carriages which carried the queen and queen mother in 1963 and Queen Elizabeth II in 1972. The museum is home to a fine collection of locomotives, the royal train, rolling stock, memorabilia, posters and interpretive displays.

The museum is also home to the Isle of Man's only railway simulator. Unveiled in summer 2016, the 'Drive the Diesel' simulator experience costs £5 for a fifteen-minute session or £10 for the enthusiast-level training. The museum also has a souvenir shop with gifts for train enthusiasts and visitors alike. The Railway Museum is open on the days the Steam Railway operates, from March to November. From here, retrace your steps to the Four Roads roundabout and pick up the road to Port St Mary.

Follow Bay View Road into the village. The one way system will take you on to Park Road and from here take a left on to Queens Road. At the bottom turn right, onto Clifton Road. On your left you will see the Isle of Man Steam Packet Company memorial at Kallow Point. The centrepiece of the monument is the anchor recovered from the wreck of the steamer *Mona's Queen*, lost at Dunkirk in 1940, and around it are recorded the names of Steam Packet personnel killed during Operation Dynamo in 1940. The memorial is the scene of an annual service of commemoration each year on 29 May, the anniversary of the sinking of the three ships concerned.

Retrace your steps back along Clifton Road and Queens Road to pick up Athol Street, heading out of the village. Turn left at Victoria Road followed by a right on to Cronk Road, before joining the Howe Road towards Cregneash. As the Howe Road reaches its highest point, some sweeping views can be

The Mona's Queen *anchor at Kallow Point. The memorial commemorates the Manx sailors lost at Dunkirk*

had back towards Port Erin, with Milner's Tower visible in the distance. Standing upon Bradda Headland overlooking Port Erin and its bay, Milner's Tower was built in 1871 by the residents of Port Erin in honour of William Milner, a Liverpool safe-maker (hence the shape of the tower in the form of a lock), who was a great benefactor to the town. Passing a thatched cottage on your right, you are now approaching **Cregneash**. As you enter the village, leave the car in the car park on the right-hand side (formerly a quarry).

Cregneash was founded relatively recently in Manx terms, and the village dates probably back only as far as the 1500s. This supposition is supported by the fact that it is sited almost entirely on marginal or poor land. The name is supposedly derived from a rock on which men returning from the shore to gather wrack (sea weed) would rest. It gained a reputation as a stronghold of Manx language and culture through the work of the Manx poet Ned Beg Hom Ruy (Edward Faragher) (1831–1908). Faragher was born into a large family of twelve children in Cregneash. At this time Manx was the only language spoken in the village, and so his mother stood out as 'the only person who could converse with strangers', due to her grasp of English. His father was one of the few people in the village who could write, and so he was called upon to compose letters on behalf of other villagers. It was from his father, known as Ned Hom Ruy in Manx, that Faragher's familiar Manx name derives – with the Manx word for 'little' being added, making it Ned Beg Hom Ruy ('Little Ned with the Red Beard'). During the 1880s or '90s Faragher met the Manchester-based German folklorist, Charles Roeder. Roeder recognised the importance of Faragher, particularly as a source of folklore and cultural knowledge, and as a speaker of Manx Gaelic, ranking him as 'one of the best vernacular conversationalists extant in the Island'. This was especially important at that time as Manx language and culture were in steep decline and in serious danger of disappearing completely, due to the dying-off of the older generation and the indifference – and often even hostility – of the youth. At this time, Manx was regarded as the language of the poor, and speaking it could only hold one back. English was seen as the language which offered more prospects, particularly as emigration was the only way in which many working-class Manx people could find their livelihood.

Later, in the twentieth century the importance of Cregneash to Manx language and culture grew, as it became one of the last strongholds of the language. The crofter Harry Kelly was believed to be the last 'native speaker' of Manx, and when he died in 1934 his cottage became the first outpost of the Manx Museum. Gradually, Manx National Heritage has acquired more property in the village, and Cregneash is revered in British museum circles as the first open-air museum in the British Isles (a concept which then Manx Museum director William Cubbon first encountered in Scandinavia). Even today, with many larger rivals such as Ironbridge or Beamish, it remains one of the few open-air museums in the British Isles in which the buildings are in situ, not transported from elsewhere to form an artificial construct.

Even though the museum is open-air, an admission fee still applies and the first thing one should do is buy a ticket from the office at Cummal Beg. Here you will also find information about special events or demonstrations which may be taking place that day, and upstairs an exhibition exploring the traditional Manx way of life and local building techniques. The buildings of Cregneash represent different crafts, different social strata and different eras within the history of the village. A good place to start your visit is with Harry Kelly's cottage. Here, as elsewhere, costumed guides are on hand to tell you more about the history of the building and its former occupant.

Harry Kelly's cottage has come to personify the simple Manx cottage, with its two front windows and centrally placed doorway opening straight into the main living space with its large open kitchen hearth ('chiollagh'). To one side a door opens into the only other room, which served as a bed space, with a half-loft above which could be used as extra sleeping accommodation or for storage. The underside of the thatched roof is open to see, with the characteristic underlay of turf 'scraa' preserved by years of peat smoke. Above this, layers of wheat straw provide an effective weatherproof seal, even against the strong winds that blow through the village. Viewed from outside, the web of ropes holding the thatch in place is a clear indication of how this local technique of thatching has been made to work despite the difficult climate.

To the south of the village and to the right of the road is a turn off which quickly becomes a track suitable only for walking, or the sturdiest of four by four vehicles. This leads up to the remains of the Cregneash radar site, a highly secret wartime installation, part of the Chain Home early-warning system, which detected bombers coming up the Irish Sea, and which passed the information the the RAF's 9 Group command centre at Preston. Today the main features still visible are pill boxes. The mounds which would have been machine gun positions, and the concrete bases of the radar buildings themselves are also evident. With more diligent searching, you may also be able to discern the smaller concrete anchor points for the guy ropes which supported the masts among the heather. Part of this site remained operational into the Cold War, with Royal Navy radar attempting to detect Soviet submarines on the seabed, but when this was finally abandoned the Ministry of Defence comprehensively destroyed the concrete structures (and presumably any remaining equipment) with explosives. From the radar site, follow the footpath northwards for another couple of hundred feet. This will take you to the **Meayll Circle**, at the summit of Meayll Hill. The circle is a chambered cairn that is believed to have been built in the Neolithic age; within this archaeological monument you will find twelve burial chambers in an 18ft ring, with six entrance passages leading into each pair of chambers. Over time it has become the site of many legends connecting it with Viking and medieval times, as well as supernatural events.

Allow one-and-a-half to two hours to see Cregneash properly (more if you are planning to explore the radar site). After that, if time (and the weather) permits, follow the winding road down to the Sound, and take in often spectacular views of the Calf of Man as you do so. The Calf takes its name from the Norse term *Kalfr,* literally the calf of a cow or whale, indicating the relationship of the smaller islet to the main island. The tides rushing through the Sound are treacherous, and many ships have come to grief in these waters. As you walk down to the cliff edge the Thousla Cross is immediately apparent, commemorating the loss of the French ship *Jeune St Charles* here in 1858. A contemporary account records that the schooner slipped her anchor in a violent storm and was dragged into the Sound:

> The boat was launched with the hope of saving life, and the master and crew, numbering six in all got into her but in a minute both the schooner and punt were in the breakers on the Thousla Rock. The schooner stuck fast, but the punt was upset; four of the crew got hold of the top of the rock, which was only to be seen every receding wave: the two lads were swept away and drowned. After the four men had spent about three hours in this position, a boat came close

to the rock ... but the breakers were still violent; and the men could not avail themselves of a line that was thrown to them. These undaunted men knowing that the tide was ebbing, and that their rescue would be effected with less risk by and by, went into a creek on the Calf, and gave information of the wreck to the light keepers. In the meantime another boat came from the mainland [and] effected the rescue one by one by means of a rope which was passed from the rock to the boat. The rock being nearer to the Calf Island than to the mainland, and the sea being less violent on that side, they were landed there and conveyed to the Light Towers, where their wounds were dressed and their wants attended to in a manner beyond all praise. The poor fellows were seriously injured and almost in a state of nudity.[34]

The original Thousla Cross was an iron Cross of Lorraine and was set on top of a beacon on Thousla Rock. It was constructed by the Northern Lighthouse Board following the loss of the *Jeune St Charles* to provide a refuge, where shipwrecked mariners could remain out of reach of wind and sea. The beacon was completed in 1859 and the cross was paid for by monies raised in France. The beacon and the cross were destroyed in November 1905, and it was not until 1907 that the Northern Lighthouse Board awarded a Port St Mary firm a contract to build a concrete structure on Thousla Rock. This structure is still there today and has the Admiralty Lights Reference A4745. On top of the concrete structure, Mr Willie Collister placed a double cross made of red wood.

In 1980 the wooden cross was removed and replaced by a gas light to give better warning to shipping in the area. At this time the Rushen Parish Commissioners decided that the circumstances surrounding the wreck of the *Jeune St Charles*, the loss of life and great bravery in the final rescue should be commemorated in the re-erection of the Thousla Cross on the Sound mainland, at its nearest point to the Thousla Rock.

Perhaps the most famous shipwreck to have occurred here is that of the brig *Lily*, which took place a few years earlier in 1852. The *Lily* was carrying a cargo which included gunpowder bound for West Africa when she ran aground in the Sound. It is believed that an initial search party left a candle burning in the hold, and when some time later a second salvage party went aboard her to attempt to rescue some of the cargo, the gunpowder exploded with tremendous force. Most of the salvage party – all local men – were killed, and it is reported that burning debris rained down as far away as Cregneash. Indeed, some of the thatched roofs in the village were set alight by it.

If you intend to make a visit to the Calf itself, then a boat crossing must be arranged. A number of local boats operate trips from either Port Erin or Port St Mary. It is possible to make a day visit to the Calf, though many people opt to stay at the Bird Observatory operated by Manx National Heritage (be warned, facilities are basic!). Details of how to book can be found on the Manx National Heritage website. There are some interesting historical features on the Calf. In the early Christian period, it was home to a hermit or monk, as evidenced by the magnificent Calf of Man crucifixion stone which must once have been an altar frontal. A number of sites on the Calf have been put forward as the possible location of his Keeill.

The historic Sound and Calf of Man; many ships have come to grief in these treacherous waters, whilst the islet has been home to several fascinating characters

In the Middle Ages there was regular traffic between the locals on the main island and the Calf, for the purposes of collecting the young of the Manx Shearwater, which nests in burrows in the ground. These chicks tasted so strongly of fish that the Catholic church gave permission for them to be eaten on a Friday. In the Jacobean era the islet is purported to have been home to Thomas Bushell, who had been exiled here from court between 1628 and 1630. He was a protege of the Lord Chancellor Francis Bacon, and was responsible for developing mining under licence from the king. In his own words:

> The embrions of my mines proving abortive by the sudden fall and death of my late Lord Chancellor Bacon, in King James's reign, were the motives which persuaded my pensive retirement to a three years unsociable solitude in a desolate Island, called the Calf of Man, where, in obedience to my dead lord's philosophic advice, I resolved to make a perfect experiment upon myself for the obtaining of a long and healthy life, most necessary for such a repentance, as my former debauchedness required, by a parsimonious diet of herbs, oil, mustard, and honey, with water sufficient, most like to that our long-lived fathers before the flood, as was conceived by that lord, which I most strictly observed, as if obliged by a religious vow, till Divine Providence called me to a more active life.[35]

Again, there are a number of possible locations for Bushell's house. Some years later during the English Civil War, James Stanley fortified the Calf, placing a half-moon battery of cannon there, overlooking the Sound. In 1644 the battery was set up on the Burroo, a rock separated from the Calf by Gull y Burroo. In 1818 the Northern Lighthouse Board constructed two lighthouses on the Calf, and for many years these were permanently manned, before being superseded by an automated facility in the 1960s. The impressive structures remain, however, and are now bird sanctuaries.

Leaving Port Erin via the Castletown Road, if time permits you can deviate left on to the A29 and then left again towards Ballafesson to view the remains of the motte and bailey castle at **Cronk Howe Mooar,** which is believed to be one of the castles built by Magnus Barelegs, in the style which the Normans used in their conquest of England around the same time. If you continue on to Reayrt Y Cronk and then Honna Road this will enable you to see the fort from the road, with a stile in front of you and a mobile phone mast behind in the distance. The fort exists now only as a mound of earth. Retrace your steps and join the A7 heading east towards Colby. This road will take you past Arbory church on the left-hand side of the road, which contains the grave of Captain John Quilliam. Further on, in Ballabeg, a large farm (private property) on the right-hand side of the road incorporates the buildings of the medieval **Bemaken Friary**. William de Montecute, Earl of Salisbury and King of Mann, petitioned Pope Urban V to allow the introduction to the Island of the Franciscan Friars. The Pope agreed to the construction of a church or oratory, with a bell tower, bell, cemetery, houses and other necessary offices. The friary was built around 1373, on an older Celtic site, and dissolved by Henry VIII at the time of the Reformation.

Continue to follow the A7 towards Ballasalla. It will take you directly past Rushen Abbey, if you have not already had a chance to visit. In Ballasalla, rejoin the A5 heading northwards towards Douglas. After passing the Mann Cat Sanctuary on the right, shortly we come to the hamlet of Newtown. Nearby lies the **Broogh Fort,** which may be one of the other motte and bailey forts built by King Magnus. If you wish to investigate it, turn left just past the bus stop onto Moaney Road. Continue to follow this road until you pass a minor cross roads. The fort is on your right. Afterwards, rejoin the A5 to return to Douglas.

Notes

1. *Journal of the Manx Museum* Vol 7 no 86 1970, p.145
2. Killings, Douglas B., *Njal's Saga*, sl, 1995
3. *Chronica Regum Mannie et Insularum* (*The Chronicles of the Kings of Man and the Isles*). *A facsimile of the manuscript Codex Julius A. VII. in the British Museum,* Douglas, 1924
4. ibid
5. Morrison, Sophia, *Manx Fairy Tales* London, 1911, p.154
6. ibid
7. *Manx Society vol 7 'Monumenta de Insula Manniae – Vol 2*' pp.183/184
8. Moore, A.W., *A History of the Isle of Man* London, 1900, p.214
9. *Bradshaw's Manchester Journal* Vol 1 1841
10. Moore, A.W., *The Folklore of the Isle of Man* Douglas, 1891, p.81
11. Bullock, Hannah, *History of the Isle of Man* London, 1816, p.211
12. Moore, T.M., *Isle of Man Natural History and Antiquarian Society Proceedings* Vol 74 p.686
13. ibid
14. *Manks Advertiser* January 1812
15. Forrest, Katherine, *Manx Recollections,* Douglas 1894, p.26
16. *Manx Quarterly* 1913
17. Bradbury, J, *Dr Bradbury's Guide to Laxey* sl, 1875
18. Walker, Mick, *Bob McIntyre the Flying Scot* Stoke on Trent, 2006, p.115
19. Davison, G.S., *Racing Reminiscences: By Riders of the Past and Present* Birmingham, 1948, p.69
20. Fogarty, Carl, *Foggy: The Explosive Autobiography* London, 2001, p.157
21. *The Motor Cycle* 29 June 1939 p.370
22. Cohen-Portheim, Paul, *Time Stood Still* London, 1931, p.32
23. Manx National Heritage MS 10423
24. Pertwee, Jon, *Moon Boots and Dinner Suits* London, 1984, p.183
25. *The Oracle and Public Advertiser* 20 February 1796
26. Manx National Heritage, Folklife Survey, David Borland FLS B/006-A

27. Gillow, Dean, *Our Lady of the Sea and St Maughold* sl, 1910
28. *Isle of Man Times* 18 September 1959
29. *Manx Quarterly* no 26, 1921
30. *Mannin* #1, 1913
31. *Isle of Man Weekly Times* 30 November 1962
32. Manx National Heritage, Folklife Survey, Annie Clague FLS C/033-A
33. *Isle of Man Examiner,* 3 September 1926
34. *Manx Sun*, 17 April 1858
35. Roeder, Charles, *Manx Notes and Queries* Douglas, 1904, p.62

Bibliography and Further Reading

Bradbury, J., *Dr Bradbury's Guide to Laxey* sl, 1875
Bullock, Hannah, *History of the Isle of Man* London, 1816
Cohen-Portheim, Paul, *Time Stood Still* London, 1931
Copparelli, Paul and Mylchreest, Peter, *Isle of Man TT Circuit Memorials Revealed* Douglas, 2009
Cresswell, Yvonne *Living With the Wire* Douglas, 1994
Davison, G.S., *Racing Reminiscences: By Riders of the Past and Present* Birmingham, 1948
Fogarty, Carl, *Foggy: The Explosive Autobiography* London, 2001
Francis, Paul, *Isle of Man 20th century Military Archaeology* Douglas, 2006
Gardner, Gerald, *Witchcraft Today* London,1954
Johnson, Andrew and Fox, Allison, *A Guide to the Archaeological Sites of the Isle of Man*, Douglas, 2017
Kermode, P.M.C., *Manx Crosses* London, 1907
Killings, Douglas B., *Njal's Saga* sl, 1995
Marshall, W.L., *The Calf of Man* Isle of Man, 1978
Moore, A.W., *The Folklore of the Isle of Man* London, 1891
Moore, A. W., *A History of the Isle of Man* London, 1900
Morrison, Sophia, *Manx Fairytales* London, 1911
Pertwee, Jon, *Moon Boots and Dinner Suits* London, 1984
Richardson, Matthew, *This Terrible Ordeal,* Douglas, 2013
Richardson, Matthew, *Isle of Man at War 1939-45* Barnsley, 2018
Walker, Mick, *Bob McIntyre the Flying Scot* Stoke on Trent, 2006
Wint, Andy, *Manx Giant from the Wonderful Isle of Man: The Story of Radio Caroline North 1964–1968* Douglas, 2008

Index

Agostini, Giacomo, 63

Ballacraine, 64, 116, 118
Baillie-Scott, Mackay Hugh, 57, 104, 134
Bee Gees, 87–8, 117
Bishopscourt, 27, 115–6
Bligh, William, 31–2, 100
Bronze Age, 2–5, 16, 115, 118, 136

Calf of Man, 6, 9, 129, 140–3
Camera Obscura, 45–6
Castle Mona, 34–5, 132
Castle Rushen, 15, 17–9, 25–6, 39, 134, 136
Castletown, 7, 19, 21, 29, 37–40, 47, 57, 61, 80, 82, 87, 89, 96, 118, 127, 131–6, 143
Christian, Fletcher, 32–3, 98, 102
Cregneash, 1, 54–6, 80, 92, 137–40, 142
Crovan, Godred (King Orry), 12–3, 15–6, 112, 121
Crow, Hugh, 33

Douglas, 6, 12–5, 19, 21, 26, 30–4, 36–41, 43–7, 53, 57–9, 61, 71, 77–9, 84, 86–7, 90–2, 95–104, 106, 116–8, 130–2, 144
Druid's Circle, 2
Dunlop, Joey, 63, 68–9

English Civil War, 25–9, 100, 113, 134, 143

First World War, 43, 63, 74, 79, 123–4
Fogarty, Carl, 65
Forde, Florrie, 78, 127
Formby, George, 62, 78–9, 92, 100

Gardner, Gerald, 89, 136
Gaiety theatre, 44–5, 86, 103
Groudle Glen, 48–9
Grove museum, 53–4, 112

Hailwood, Mike, 67, 69, 71
Hall Caine, Thomas Henry, 56–7
Hill forts, 3–4, 7, 130
Honda, Soichiro, 63
Horse trams, 46, 90, 95, 102
House of Manannan, 11, 53, 119, 123

Internment, 75–6, 79, 85, 95, 102, 123
Iron Age, 4–5, 7, 130

Kerroogarrow, 26, 28, 113
King Orry's Grave, 1, 109
Knockaloe, 75–7, 123–5
Knox, Archibald, 57–8, 98–100

Lag ny Keeilley, 6, 128–9
Laxey, 48, 50, 51–3, 69, 71, 104–9
Leece Museum, 53, 123

Magnus Barefoot, 15–7, 143–4
Manx Aviation and Military Museum, 85
Manx Electric Railway, 46–7, 106

Manx Heritage Transport Museum, 48, 113
Manx Museum, 6, 8, 12, 14, 30, 34, 36, 53, 55–6, 58, 95, 100, 105, 119, 128, 139
Martin, Guy, 64, 92
Meayll Circle, 1, 140
Mesolithic, 1, 7, 133
Milntown, 14, 28, 67, 98, 111–2
Morrison, Sophia, 20, 126

Nautical Museum, 38, 134–5
Niarbyl, 30, 78, 81, 83, 92, 125–8

Old Grammar School, 21, 134
Old House of Keys, 37–8, 96, 135

Pankhurst, Emmeline, 59
Peel, 6, 12–3, 15–7, 19, 26, 46–7, 53, 57, 61, 75, 116–7, 119–23, 126–7, 136
Peel Castle, 15–7, 26, 119–21, 127
Pertwee, Jon, 86
Port Erin, 18, 46–7, 136, 138, 142–3
Port St Mary, 126, 136, 141–2

Quilliam, John, 36–8, 95, 135–6, 144

Radar, 69, 80–1, 83–4, 86, 102, 125, 139, 140
Radio Caroline, 91, 111

Ramsey, 12, 26–8, 33, 43, 46–7, 50, 53–4, 67–8, 91, 98, 104, 106, 109–12, 115, 118, 136
Robert the Bruce, 18, 23
Ronaldsway, 2, 4, 22–3, 47, 83–5, 113, 133
Rushen Abbey, 15, 18–9, 21, 77, 132, 144

St George's church, 32, 39–42, 96–8
St Trinian's chapel, 19–20, 118
Schwitters, Kurt, 79–80
Second World War, 45, 48, 67, 79, 85, 87, 112, 114, 125, 133–4
Sheene, Barry, 63
Ship burials, 6–7, 136
Sky Hill, 12–3, 112
Slavery, 8, 32–4, 117
Smuggling, 30, 97, 100
Sound, the, 5, 9, 140–3
South Barrule, 3–4, 130
Stanley, James (7th Earl of Derby), 25–8, 122, 134, 143

Tower of Refuge, 40–1
Tynwald Hill, 9–10, 118

Villa Marina, 44–5

Walker, Murray, 71
Wisdom, Norman, 92
Woods, Stanley, 67

Dear Reader,

We hope you have enjoyed this book, but why not share your views on social media? You can also follow our pages to see more about our other products: facebook.com/penandswordbooks or follow us on Twitter @penswordbooks

You can also view our products at www.pen-and-sword.co.uk (UK and ROW) or www.penandswordbooks.com (North America).

To keep up to date with our latest releases and online catalogues, please sign up to our newsletter at: www.pen-and-sword.co.uk/newsletter

If you would like a printed catalogue with our latest books, then please email: enquiries@pen-and-sword.co.uk or telephone: 01226 734555 (UK and ROW) or email: Uspen-and-sword@casematepublishers.com or telephone: (610) 853-9131 (North America).

We respect your privacy and we will only use personal information to send you information about our products.

Thank you!